C000078670

word for **TODAY**

Tested by FIRE

Daniel 1-6: Solid faith in today's world

CHRIS WRIGHT

SCRIPTURE UNION
130 CITY ROAD, LONDON EC1V 2NJ

© Chris Wright 1993

First published 1993
by Scripture Union, 130 City Road, London EC1V 2NJ
ISBN 0 86201 846 3

All rights reserved. No part of this publication may be reproduced, stored
in a retrieval system, or transmitted, in any form or by any means,
electronic, mechanical, photocopying, recording or otherwise, without the
prior permission of Scripture Union.

The right of Chris Wright to be identified as author of this work has been
asserted by him in accordance with the Copyright, Designs and Patents
Act 1988.

British Library Cataloguing-in-Publication Data
A catalogue record for this book is available from the British Library

Unless otherwise specified, Scripture quotations in this publication are
from the Holy Bible, New International Version, Copyright © 1973, 1978,
1984 International Bible Society, published by Hodder and Stoughton.

Phototypeset by Intype, London.

Printed and bound in Great Britain by
Cox and Wyman Ltd, Reading.

CONTENTS

INTRODUCTION

After giving up my childhood attempts to learn the piano properly, I found as a teenager that I could play it by ear and made great strides by playing for all the songs and choruses in our Belfast church youth group in the early Sixties – murdering most of the tunes by playing them all in the only two or three keys I had mastered. One old Negro spiritual was very popular and very easy for a ham pianist like me to play.

> This world is not my home, I'm just a-passin'
>   through.
> My treasure is laid up, somewhere beyond the blue.
> The angels beckon me from heaven's open door,
> And I can't feel at home in this world any more.

I enjoyed playing the catchy tune, but that was partly because it got me out of having to sing the words. Because, frankly, I didn't like them at all. They seemed sloppy and only half true. Knowing nothing of the suffering and oppression out of which such words arose, they seemed sheer escapism to my youthful idealism. This world *is* my home, I remember thinking, and God has put me here for a purpose. So the angels can go and beckon somebody else if they want – I'm staying.

And yet, of course, the song is partly right. This world *is* alien territory for the Christian in one sense: not planet earth itself, which is part of God's good creation, but 'the world' as it is sometimes described in the Bible – the world of humanity organized without reference to God, or in rebellion against him; the world as a place of fallen-ness and curse, of evil and sin. *That* is a world we have been saved from and yet still have to live in. So in a sense, yes, we are 'passing through' it. The language of pilgrimage has a good pedigree in the Bible. We are on a journey to somewhere better, though the Bible describes it as not just heaven and angels, but as a whole new creation, a new heaven and a new earth. So we are living *in* this world, but in the light of a destiny that lies beyond it.

The New Testament puts a sharp edge on this tension by talking about the kingdom of God in contrast and conflict with the kingdom of Satan, or the kingdoms of this world. This is the primary tension that the Christian has to live with. We are 'in the world but not of it' – at home in the world because it is still God's world, yet alienated from the world because the world is so alienated from God. How then can the believer live as a citizen of the kingdom of God while having to live in an earthly kingdom? More specifically, how can the believer witness to his or her faith (or preserve it at all) in the midst of an alien and non-Christian culture, whether that means the culture of some other religion (eg, in Islamic countries), or the culture of the secular, increasingly pagan West? Especially, how can the believer do this if it involves a high cost in misunderstanding, suffering, threat, or even death?

I have been told by some Christians in India, in all seriousness, that it is simply impossible to be in business and maintain fully biblical standards of integrity. Whatever you may *want* to do, business simply cannot function without the bribery and corruption that goes on behind the scenes, or even on the open stage. Others have told me that it *is* possible, but only with a lot of faith and courage. Teachers in Britain point to the climate of hostility and sometimes the threat of disciplinary action that hangs over any overt Christian faith commitment that can be smeared with charges of indoctrination or intolerance. The only thing one can be dogmatic about in our culture is the prime virtue of not being dogmatic about anything, especially not in front of the children. A Christian woman gave up her job when it became clear that among the expectations of her employers was that she should accept the sexual advances of business clients as part of the process of bargaining for contracts. In some parts of India, Christians who refuse to participate in neighbourhood Hindu festivals or to contribute financially to them, face personal intimidation and serious vandalism against their homes and property.

Such issues are not new. Christians have faced them ever since Nero's lions, and even before that. Jews also have faced the same questions all through their history. So it is not surprising that the Hebrew Bible (or Old Testament, as Christians call it) gives a lot of attention to these questions. The book of Daniel tackles the problem head on, both in the stories of Daniel and his friends, and in the visions he received. A major theme of the book is how people who worship the one, true, living God – the God of Israel – can live and work and survive in the midst of a nation, a culture and a government that are hostile and sometimes life-threatening. And that will be our focus in this book.

Daniel, of course, has been used for many other purposes, especially by those with a gift for arithmetic and a fascination for describing the end of the world in advance. That is not our concern here. People who go in for complicated biblical arithmetic always seem to have to revise their sums. In any case the New Testament tells us that the end of the world will be a surprising and unpredictable event, perhaps most of all for those who have it timetabled so precisely. Recent events in Europe and the former Soviet Union have certainly upset the calculations of some whose confident predictions had been partly based on the visions of Daniel. So we shall leave the future-gazing to the astrologers and magicians like the ones who cross the stage of the book of Daniel with such contemptible futility, and wrestle instead with the question of survival in the here and now, as Daniel and his three friends did.

1

COMPROMISE

OR

CONFRONTATION?

The world was falling apart. So it must have seemed to people who lived through the events that are summarized in Daniel 1.

> In the third year of the reign of Jehoiakim king of Judah, Nebuchadnezzar king of Babylon came to Jerusalem and besieged it. And the Lord delivered Jehoiakim king of Judah into his hand, along with some of the articles from the temple of God. These he carried off to the temple of his god in Babylonia and put in the treasure-house of his god.
>
> *Daniel 1:1, 2*

This reads like a straightforward statement of fact, but it leaves a lot unsaid that needs to be filled in a little for the modern reader if we are going to feel the impact of the shattering events that lie behind the book.

CLASH OF EMPIRES

It was the year 609 BC. In the Middle East, like Europe in the 1990s, a sprawling empire was falling apart and new power blocks were forming. Assyria had ruled the world for 150 years – a century and a half of strong, centralized, military rule which had submerged many a small nation in its ruthless conquests. Among the small nations that had been destroyed was the northern kingdom of Israel itself, which had been smashed and scattered to the winds just over a hundred years earlier in 721 BC. Jerusalem and the southern kingdom of Judah had been spared that fate, but had been little more than a subject, satellite country in Assyria's empire for well over a century.

But now Assyria itself was collapsing. The new rising power was Babylon under the energetic leadership of a youthful king, Nebuchadnezzar. The great western power, Egypt, sensed that the time was right for an attempt to re-establish their power, so the Egyptian king, Pharaoh Necho, marched with his army up through Palestine with the intention of helping Assyria against the Babylonian threat. The king in Judah at the time was Josiah. He had no desire to see any delay in the much longed-for collapse of the hated Assyrian empire, so he marched out to try to stop Necho coming to their assistance. It was a well intentioned but futile gesture. His hopelessly outnumbered army met the Egyptians at Megiddo (near Mount Carmel) and was defeated. Josiah himself was slain in battle, and Pharaoh Necho captured Josiah's son and heir, Shallum (also called Coniah), and deported him off to Egypt. Necho then installed Jehoiakim on the throne in Jerusalem –

the king mentioned here in Daniel 1:1.

Nebuchadnezzar managed to beat off the Egyptian attempt to strip the carcass of the Assyrian empire. He conclusively defeated Egypt at the battle of Carchemish in 605 BC. Babylon thus became the dominant power in Mesopotamia and the whole of west Asia, and remained so for about the next seventy years. So it was the end of an era and the beginning of a new one. Smaller states in the region had to dance to the Babylonian tune, and Judah was one of those small states. Shortly after his victory at Carchemish, Nebuchadnezzar came south and threatened Jerusalem. On that occasion he took a small number of captives off to Babylon, probably as hostages to ensure the good behaviour of the vassal state.

Among these early exiles were Daniel and his three friends, who must have been only teenagers at the time. Probably they would have been in training for religious or government service in Jerusalem, destined, they must have thought, for the peaks of serving the people of God in the city of David. Instead, without warning, they found themselves a thousand miles from home, torn away from everything they knew and dumped down in a pagan, gentile, enemy state. All around them were foreign people, a strange language, an alien culture and, worst of all, gods and idols galore. It must have been a horrifying and traumatic experience. Worse was to come.

FAITH IN THE MIDST OF A HISTORICAL CRISIS

Why had all this happened? Verse 2 gives a breath-takingly blunt answer: 'the Lord' – that is, Yahweh, the God of Israel – 'delivered Jehoiakim into Nebuchadnez-zar's hand.'

God did it! Well of course he did, we say. It's obvious, because we've read the prophets and they kept telling the people of Israel that God was going to punish them through their enemies. We can look back on the story with the benefit of hindsight. But at the time most of the people were in the habit of ignoring the prophets, and the whole confusion of events in those years must have seemed inconceivable. People had a whole raft of questions as they tried to make sense out of current events. How could the God of Israel allow his people to be treated like this? Had Yahweh met his match? Were the gods of Babylon actually younger and stronger? Would it not be more sensible then to go with the flow and switch to worshipping the gods of Babylon? Or if, as some prophets (especially Jeremiah) were saying, it really was Yahweh who had done this, wasn't he being unfair and unjust? (Ezekiel tackled this complaint in Ezekiel 18.)

And – perhaps the hardest question facing those who had accepted the word of the prophets that God had indeed done this – was there now any hope for the future? If God had poured out his judgment on Israel, was there anything left to look forward to? And what about God's purposes *through* Israel? The Israelites believed God had made them into a nation to use them for the blessing of the rest of the nations. This was built into the promise God had made to Abraham (Genesis 12:1–3), and was the reason why God had built up such a close relationship with Israel. This was the point of the presence of God in his temple, and the deeper meaning of all the holy objects which formed part of its furniture. God was the God of Israel in order that he could ultimately show he was God of all the earth. Many of the psalms sung in the temple celebrated this belief. So what were the people to make of the fact that these very objects associated with the worship of the living God had been taken off by a pagan king and, worse still, been placed in the temple of *his* god!? And that pagan temple was in the land of 'Shinar' – that is, the same place as the Tower of Babel (Genesis 11:1–9). It was like some ghastly time-warp, as if God had put history in reverse and gone back before Abraham was even heard of. Something was surely very, very wrong. Either their whole system of belief was mistaken, or events had got out of control.

It seemed that an enormous chasm had opened up between their faith on the one hand and world events on the other, so that events seemed utterly to contradict their faith. And so they came to the final, crunch question – is God really still in control? When catastrophe strikes, is God still sovereign? Are we able to accept God's freedom to act as he chooses, even when he does something that seems to contradict his own purposes or, at least, something that runs right against what *we* thought was his will?

It was not hard for Christians to talk about the hand of God in the collapse of European communist dictatorships and the fall of the Berlin Wall in 1989–90. It was not so easy, however, for Christians to understand why God allowed the Iron Curtain to be imposed in the first place; especially difficult for those who thought the horrific cost of the Second World War worth paying to free Europe from one tyranny, only to see it being replaced by another. How could events back then be reconciled with the will of God?

More pointedly, if we believe God has commissioned Christians to spread the gospel, and that it is God's purpose that the church should witness and grow in every nation, how can we reconcile this with the fact that he allows so many countries to close their doors to Christian missionaries, and to restrict or ban Christian activities? When communist China expelled missionaries in the early 1950s, it sent shock waves through the Christian church, since China was one of the largest 'mission fields' of that era. If you have a theology that says God wants mission, that God is in control of the world, how can you cope when you have to stand by and watch as God allows mission to be squashed in the largest nation on earth? Well, again with hindsight, we can see that the end of *Western* missions in China did not mean the end of *mission* in China, nor did it mean the end of the church there. We can see all that *now*, but it was a shattering blow at the time.

And in personal life, it can be a severe struggle when the things we believe about God and his will for our lives are flatly contradicted by the circumstances he puts us through. A student at All Nations, who came with a proven record of overseas work and with fine intentions of further training, fell into a prolonged period of clinical depression, fuelled by a whole mixture of 'unfinished business' from the past. The worst part of it, the deepest pit as she described it, was when she found it hard to go on believing in her heart all the things about God himself that she knew in her head. Faith and reality were just too far apart. It *almost* came to the point where God just became too unbelievable because of what he had allowed to happen to her – if he really had.

The book of Daniel opens, then, with just this sort of contradiction between faith and facts. It goes on to show us the response of a few young men who lived through it, yet who managed not only to survive but to adjust to the new facts and maintain the integrity of their faith. Their God, they were able to affirm, was still in control, even in a world that seemed out of control.

FAITH IN THE MIDST OF A PERSONAL CRISIS

The international crisis that had engulfed their world also hurled Daniel and his friends into a cultural and personal crisis that tested them severely, even though they were so young at the time. They had to face not merely the fact of *living* in Babylon, but also the demand that they enter the service of its political administration. This was due to Nebuchadnezzar's government policy.

> Then the king ordered Ashpenaz, chief of his court officials, to bring in some of the Israelites from the royal family and the nobility – young men without any physical defect, handsome, showing aptitude for every kind of learning, well informed, quick to

understand, and qualified to serve in the king's palace. He was to teach them the language and literature of the Babylonians. The king assigned them a daily amount of food and wine from the king's table. They were to be trained for three years, and after that they were to enter the king's service.

Among these were some from Judah: Daniel, Hananiah, Mishael and Azariah.   *Daniel 1:3–6*

Nebuchadnezzar had a relatively enlightened sort of programme very different from the harsh Assyrian regime that had gone before. He decided to give a cultural re-education to the cream of the populations he had conquered, and then employ them in the service of his new and growing state. It may have been rather like the way the British empire provided English education for an elite among 'the natives' in countries like India, so that there could be a class of competent administrators to cope with routine civil affairs under the imperial government. Nebuchadnezzar was specific about the kind of people he wanted. They would be physically and intellectually equipped for service. Daniel and his friends had those qualities – qualities that would have destined them for the service of God in Jerusalem, but now, by the cruel twist of history, at the disposal of the king who was soon to destroy Jerusalem.

Nebuchadnezzar's civil service diploma course lasted three years and involved four elements: education in Babylonian culture; state maintenance; a career in the political administration of the state; substitution of Babylonian names for Jewish ones. For young Jewish men, brought up in Jerusalem, it called for a huge cultural change and re-orientation. They must have wrestled hard with their consciences as they came to decisions about how to respond. Could they accept these new arrangements? Would they be compromising their faith or committing idolatry by submitting to such a programme?

Did they have a choice anyway? Well, yes. They could have chosen the path of total refusal, which might have ended in martyrdom. Then they might have gone down in history among the long line of those who have died for their faith and convictions. It wasn't that they lacked the courage for such a course because later, in Daniel 3 and 6, we find that all four of them on different occasions were prepared to die if necessary. But instead, we find that they accepted three out of the four requirements. Most sermons I ever heard on this chapter of Daniel in my youth emphasized the negative refusal, the courageous stand of Daniel and Co. The preachers and Bible study leaders never commented on the remarkable degree of *acceptance* that they showed. Three times they said 'Yes', before they said 'No'.

They said 'Yes' to a pagan education

They were to be taught all 'the language and literature of the Babylonians' (Daniel 1:4b). That is, they were to have a complete re-education in Babylonian culture and civilization. Now the Mesopotamian civilization was one of the greatest of the ancient world. It had made great advances in literature, mathematics, astronomy and primitive science. But it was also riddled with all the features of polytheism – ie a religion with many gods and idols. It was full of magic and occult practices,

19

and particularly 'rich' in astrology with all the superstitions that accompany that ancient pseudo-science. So a Babylonian education was definitely a mixed bag. Much of it could be approved, but much of it, from the viewpoint of Jewish monotheism, would have been distasteful to say the least, and downright offensive and blasphemous at worst.

Yet these young Jewish teenagers not only applied themselves to it, but even gained distinctions and got higher final results in their oral examinations than their Babylonian peers!

> To these four young men God gave knowledge and understanding of all kinds of literature and learning. And Daniel could understand visions and dreams of all kinds.
>
> At the end of the time set by the king to bring them in, the chief official presented them to Nebuchadnezzar. The king talked with them, and he found none equal to Daniel, Hananiah, Mishael and Azariah; so they entered the king's service. In every matter of wisdom and understanding about which the king questioned them, he found them ten times better than all the magicians and enchanters in his whole kingdom.   *Daniel 1:17–20*

The fact that in the following chapters we find them standing firm in their faith and resisting idolatry must mean that their childhood grounding in the faith of Israel was strong enough to cope with Babylon's university course objectively and critically. They could learn all that it had to teach them, but they didn't have to believe all it assumed. They could master its content without swallowing its falsehood. And the education they excelled in gave them access to positions in society and government from which they were able to have remarkable influence.

There is a line of thinking among some Christians that Christians ought to have a completely separate educational system. It is said that the secular, humanist assumptions on which our Western schools and universities are built don't fit with a biblical view of truth. So we should either educate our children at home, or support Christian schools where the whole curriculum would be structured on a biblical basis. I know people who believe this and act upon it, and I respect their views, but I can't agree with them.

It seems to me that what really counts is not to protect young people from the secular paganism of our culture by withdrawing them from all contact with it, but to teach them how, from a position of faith and knowledge, they can interact with it and distinguish what is good and what is evil. *That* is the job of the Christian home and the church, a job in which we sadly often fail. For how can Christians make biblical truth relevant to the needs and questions of our pagan culture unless they understand it as well as the gospel? I have always been grateful that our children, three of whom are now at university, spent part of their education in Indian schools, rubbing shoulders with Hindus, Sikhs and Muslims, and part in a British sixth-form, mixing with the usual crop of agnostics, sceptics and atheists (pupils and staff!) that one finds in a sixth-form. They brought home many a question to hammer out over our evening meal. They had to defend their own beliefs and stand up for their own choices and values. But I think they are better equipped to be salt and light in our secular world than if they had had an exclusively 'Christian education'.

They said 'Yes' to a political career

They knew that they were being groomed for government, but whose government? Not merely the government of a pagan nation, with its idolatry and its arrogance, but specifically Babylon, a nation which had already been the target of several speeches by Israel's prophets predicting that it was heading for God's judgment! In particular, they would be serving Nebuchadnezzar – the king who had snatched them from home and who would soon attack Jerusalem again to finally destroy it altogether. How could they possibly accept a job serving such a king and country? Yet they did. In fact, they were prepared to regard their service of the government as a way of serving God himself – as they later told Nebuchadnezzar to his face when he was threatening to cremate them alive (Daniel 3:17). Perhaps they drew encouragement from the stories of Joseph who likewise had served a pagan king. Or perhaps they reflected on how Obadiah had held high office under the reign of Ahab and Jezebel in spite of their blatant idolatry and evil (1 Kings 18:1–14).

There are Christians who say that Christians should not get involved in politics. It is an ambiguous world, full of half-truths, corruption and back-scratching; and if we know that the world in general and our nation in particular stand under God's judgment, what is the point of playing party games on a sinking ship? Again, I believe the Bible cuts across this kind of withdrawal syndrome. God rules the world, not just the church, and Christians, to be the light of the world, must be more than altar candles. I have a sense of gratitude and admiration for Christians in politics, especially Members of Parliament. It is a job where a man or woman's resources are stretched to the limit with constant demands on mind, body, emotions and conscience. It was partly out of a sense of solidarity with such fellow believers that I decided some years ago to join a political party myself and get involved locally, adding at least one little grain of salt to the much needed Christian influence in Britain's faltering democracy.

They said 'Yes' to a change of name

Names don't mean as much to us as they did to the ancient world. Then your whole person could be bound up in your name, and certainly names could be clues to ethnic and religious identity, as they still are in many parts of the world. So when Nebuchadnezzar insisted that all his new civil servants should have suitable Babylonian names, it was particularly costly for a Jew whose name included the name of his God – Yahweh – as Hananiah and Azariah did, especially since the new names included pagan gods, adding further insult and indignity. You might have thought that *this* would have been the sticking point for these men. Surely to swop the name of the living God of Israel for the name of a pagan god was impossible for any believer! Yet once again we find they accepted it. Perhaps, with the same kind of maturity that Paul called for in relation to idols, they knew that these gods were nothing and their names were nothing; so they could swallow hard and take them on their lips and lapel badges, knowing full well that the living God of Israel was not only still *their* God, but the *only* God.

So we find a remarkable degree of acceptance of the cultural change that had been forced upon them by the action of God in history. Already they were acting in ways which fit in with what Jeremiah later told the exiles in his letter to them (Jeremiah 29), namely that they should settle down in Babylon, live, work, build and increase there; that they should *pray* for Babylon; and that they should see themselves not just as the victims of deportation but as those whom God had *sent* there. They had to rewrite their songs – 'This world (Babylon) *is* my home, I'm *not* just passing through' – and, as a result of their choice, they were able not only to serve Babylon, but in some ways to influence it and even to preserve the lives of their fellow Jews at a later stage.

They said 'No' to the king's food

But Daniel resolved not to defile himself with the royal food and wine, and he asked the chief official for permission not to defile himself this way. Now God had caused the official to show favour and sympathy to Daniel, but the official told Daniel, 'I am afraid of my lord the king, who has assigned your food and drink. Why should he see you looking worse than the other young men of your age? The king would then have my head because of you.'

Daniel then said to the guard whom the chief official had appointed over Daniel, Hananiah, Mishael and Azariah, 'Please test your servants for ten days: Give us nothing but vegetables to eat and water to drink. Then compare our appearance with that of the young men who eat the royal food and treat your servants in accordance with what you see.' So he agreed to this and tested them for ten days.

At the end of the ten days they looked healthier and better nourished than any of the young men who ate the royal food. So the guard took away their choice food and the wine they were to drink and gave them vegetables instead. *Daniel 1:8–16*

This is ridiculous! After accepting so much, why take a stand on a matter so trivial as food? When we see how much they *were* prepared to swallow, it's hard to understand why they couldn't swallow royal meat and wine as well. There have been many attempts to explain the reasons for Daniel's stand on this point. Only two kinds of explanation seem to make sense to me.

● *The food would have been unclean*, by Jewish levitical food laws; or it would have been offered to idols before reaching the palace kitchen and so have been 'contaminated'. Either way it would have been offensive to strict Jews. This explanation says that Daniel and Co decided to preserve at least one symbolic token of their Jewish identity and monotheistic faith. The food laws of Leviticus were themselves symbolic of Israel's distinctiveness from the rest of the nations. Daniel and his friends could no longer live in a separate land among their fellow Israelites, but at least they could preserve a separate diet and so make a symbolic gesture, reminding themselves regularly of their true identity and commitment to their God.

A symbolic gesture may be very unimportant in

itself, but in some situations it can have a powerful, and potentially dangerous, meaning. Splashing water on someone is a bit of fun at the beach, but if you do it in the name of Christ in some Muslim countries you could be endangering their life and your own. Singing songs may seem pretty harmless and ineffective, but the Negro spiritual with which we began is only one of a whole category of songs that grew out of the oppression of slavery, many of which kept alive the hope of eventual liberation. Some Christians wear small lapel badges or brooches with a cross, a fish or some other Christian symbol, as a way of letting their Christian identity be known in an irreligious environment or workplace. They know that since it makes a silent statement about their Christian belief, it commits them to uncompromising standards of behaviour. Sometimes Christian convictions or a Christian conscience need such symbolic expression, even if the form of the symbol is of no intrinsic importance in itself. Sometimes, the *fact* of taking a stand on something, of drawing a line somewhere, can be more important as a witness than the substance of the issue itself. Not everything that Christians have said 'No' to is necessarily evil in itself (any more than ritually unclean food was evil in itself). But a principle or a quiet witness may be expressed at the point of refusal or non-participation.

As a student I was in my college's rowing crew. Normally we never trained on a Sunday anyway, but on a few occasions we were asked to, or were needed to attend a regatta on a Sunday. I declined to do so, which was not too popular since it involved getting a substitute oarsman to take my place for just one day. (Nobody, however, came along and made a film like *Chariots of Fire* about me!) My own convictions on the nature of Sunday observance have changed somewhat since then, and I am now more concerned about the abuse of Sunday by the forces of greed and profit through unrestrained trading than by physical exercise. So I might not take the same stand now, but I am quite sure I was right to do so then, in the context of my own Christian witness and personal conscience. It was a simple statement that, though I loved the sport and could sacrifice many things for it, there was something more important in my life than rowing – which in the world of a university college boat club was near enough to blasphemy!

In India the dominant Hindu culture pervades society and Christians find themselves out of step with practices at work and in the neighbourhood which involve the recognition of Hindu deities. Sometimes this may be as harmless as giving sweets or scattering flower petals. Not to participate can lead to ostracism or physical abuse. Indian Christians take different attitudes on the question of 'where to draw the line'; but wherever it is drawn, however insignificant the thing in itself, Christians, like Daniel and his friends, have to preserve some token of that distinctiveness from the world, which ought to have much more serious moral dimensions also.

● *The food would have symbolized 'covenant-loyalty' to the king.* This explanation focuses less on what the food would have symbolized from a Jewish point of view, and more on what it would have symbolized to the authorities. Those who suggest this way of understanding Daniel's decision point out that all food would have been technically unclean in Babylon, for Babylon was an unclean, foreign land. Wine, in any case, was not forbidden by the 'unclean' laws of Leviticus, and vegetables would have been as much dedicated to a god before preparation as meat. Also it seems that their vegetarian diet lasted only while they were being trained and was not a life-long policy, since Daniel tells us of a later period of temporary abstinence from meat which implies he normally did eat it (Daniel 10:2, 3). So the objection may not have been based on the levitical food laws.

In the ancient world, sharing the food of someone's table was sometimes a way of cementing a covenant bond between people. To eat from the king's table could, therefore, have been seen as declaring total dependence on the king and total loyalty to him. It may have been this that Daniel and his friends politely refused, and would also explain better the fear that Ashpenaz had for himself and for them if they stood firm on such a refusal.

These four young Jews decided that they could and would serve Nebuchadnezzar and his state. Indeed, they would do so to the very best of their abilities. But they would not give to him or to it the loyalty and commitment that they could ultimately give only to Yahweh. *Covenant* loyalty was exclusively for God. It could not be shared with a human king, however tempting his menu and wine list. In other words, they made a vital distinction between, on the one hand, legitimate civil service of a political regime which had been appointed by God for temporary world dominion, and on the other hand, idolatrous patriotism which would give unquestioning loyalty to a human being who might easily inflate his divine *appointment* into divine *status* and claim absolute authority.

The importance of this insight and the stand they took on the basis of it is fully vindicated later (Daniel 3), when royal food became a royal furnace and they faced a far harder choice. They could not have sung that virtually idolatrous 'hymn' which generations have been brought up on:

> I vow to thee, my country, all earthly things above,
> Entire and whole and perfect, the service of my
> love . . .

Such idolatrous patriotism is akin to many other forms of loyalty which can conflict with ultimate loyalty to God himself. George Orwell defined nationalism as the 'habit of identifying with a single nation or unit, placing it beyond good and evil, and recognizing no other duty than that of advancing its interests.' That can include political parties, team spirit, company loyalty even, in Christian circles, denominational loyalties, or commitment to one kind of theological confession, or to one great and gifted leader who can do no wrong.

We need to watch our loyalties, commitments and convictions, and constantly submit them to critical examination in the light of our one final loyalty to Christ himself as Lord. Have I become over-zealous in a cause which has great value, but is not the only Christian priority? Have I become uncritical in my support for a particular public figure or organization – secular or Christian – so that I find myself being defensive and excusing even blatant mistakes or wrongdoing? Is my loyalty to the company I work for a healthy desire for its legitimate and honest success in the market place, or an unhealthy blind acceptance of whatever it demands of me, whatever it may do to others, or to principles of truth and honesty? Are my political loyalties and opinions based on prejudice or self-interest, rather than a truly biblical view of God's concerns and priorities? Am I allowing my mind to be 'conformed to this world' rather than 'transformed' into the mind of Christ?

So, Daniel and his friends took their stand courageously and courteously on where their loyalties lay, and God vindicated them. Their education continued, was successfully completed, and their careers began on a very favourable note. The last verse of the chapter is not just a footnote.

> And Daniel remained there until the first year of King
> Cyrus.   *Daniel 1:21*

It sums up both aspects of the message of this chapter. On the one hand, it points to the sovereignty of God in history. Cyrus was the king of Persia who overthrew the Babylonian empire. Thus, the empire which had destroyed Israel in the first verse of this chapter, has itself disappeared from history in the last verse – but Daniel *and his people* and their God survived.

On the other hand, it points to the personal triumph of one individual in the midst of the turmoil of his day, and the testing choices he had to make all through his life from a very early age. God is sovereign and is still in control of the world; God alone deserves our total loyalty against all competitors. These are the two great truths which shine through this chapter and will go on echoing through the rest of the book.

2
HEAD OF GOLD
OR
FEET OF CLAY

It was only a few years ago that I joined a political party. I had been interested in social and political issues for much longer than that, but what pushed me into membership of the Liberal Democrat party was being invited to speak at the Liberal Democrat Christian Forum. There I met people who were committed both to political action and to prayer and Bible study, seeking to sprinkle some salt and shed a little light onto the world of British politics. I decided it was time to put my money where my vote was and signed up – both for the party and for the Christian Forum, since it seems to me that both are vital. I know that there are similar Christian movements in the other main parties, and also that there are excellent cross-party groupings as well, such as the Movement for Christian Democracy. Christian Members of Parliament of all parties and their spouses also meet for prayer and mutual fellowship and support.

I have also been along to conferences of Christian fellowships in the worlds of banking, education, medicine and even the veterinary profession, in Britain and India, and been greatly impressed with their commitment to working out a Christian mind and a Christian witness in those spheres.

It is hard enough being a Christian believer in the secular world, but much worse to be isolated. Sometimes God does call people to a lonely position that demands a very special kind of courage. However, it is important that, if the possibility exists, we meet with other believers and wrestle together with the pressures and problems we face. We may not have the task of saving the lives of the whole civil service through one prayer meeting, as Daniel and his friends did, but we can certainly expect to achieve much more for the kingdom of God than by playing 'Lone Rangers'.

Chapter one began with an international crisis and moved on to a personal crisis. Chapter two is the other way round. It starts with a personal problem, but ends up on the stage of world history.

NEBUCHADNEZZAR AND HIS DREAM

In the second year of his reign, Nebuchadnezzar had dreams; his mind was troubled and he could not sleep. So the king summoned the magicians, enchanters, sorcerers and astrologers to tell him what he had dreamed. When they came in and stood before the king, he said to them, 'I have had a dream that troubles me and I want to know what it means.'

Then the astrologers answered the king in Aramaic, 'O king, live forever! Tell your servants the dream and we will interpret it.'

The king replied to the astrologers, 'This is what I have firmly decided: If you do not tell me what my dream was and interpret it, I will have you cut into pieces and your houses turned into piles of rubble. But if you tell me the dream and explain it, you will receive from me gifts and rewards and great honour. So tell me the dream and interpret it for me.'

Once more they replied, 'Let the king tell his servants the dream, and we will interpret it.'

Then the king answered, 'I am certain that you are trying to gain time, because you realise that this is what I have firmly decided: If you do not tell me the dream, there is just one penalty for you. You have conspired to tell me misleading and wicked things, hoping the situation will change. So then, tell me the dream, and I will know that you can interpret it for me.'

The astrologers answered the king, 'There is not a man on earth who can do what the king asks! No king, however great and mighty, has ever asked such a thing of any magician or enchanter or astrologer. What the king asks is too difficult. No-one can reveal it to the king except the gods, and they do not live among men.'

This made the king so angry and furious that he ordered the execution of all the wise men of Babylon. So the decree was issued to put the wise men to death, and men were sent to look for Daniel and his friends to put them to death.

Daniel 2:1–13

The early years of Nebuchadnezzar's reign were very active. He had to fight many campaigns to consolidate his new empire. There were several border revolts and other external threats. Somehow he had to build up his own personal prestige and stature as the new king of a new world power. It seems that all this generated in him an inner insecurity and fear, which manifested itself in troubled dreams.

A bad dream was a bad omen in ancient Babylon, particularly if it was a repeating nightmare, as the text hints. And it was especially bad if you couldn't remember it! They had massive 'dream-books', written by experts in interpreting every kind of dream you could imagine, but they were not a great deal of use if you didn't know the dream to start off with! The story doesn't make it entirely clear whether Nebuchadnezzar genuinely could not remember the dream (as happens) and wanted the magicians to tell him, or whether he could remember it perfectly well and wanted to test the abilities of his personal magic roundabout.

What is more interesting is the fact that God was involved in the subconscious life of this young pagan king. His advisors admitted that only gods could do what he was asking of them – to tell him what he had dreamt as well as interpret it for him. But Daniel later made it clear that the living God could not only reveal and interpret the dream, but also put it in his head in the first place (Daniel 2:23, 28, 45). The God of Israel, who is sovereign over history and nations, who has hitherto spoken through the mouths of his own prophets, chooses to reveal his plans for world history not to Daniel and his house-fellowship, but to a pagan king who did not even acknowledge him (yet). It is remarkable how quick Daniel was to accept this. The attitudes of many of his contemporaries to all things foreign and pagan was much more hostile. Remember who this particular foreigner was – the man who had deported him and his friends, and who, in a few more years, would destroy Jerusalem and deport most of the population to Babylon. How could God possibly 'talk' to such a man? If God had revelation to give, why not use one of his own people? The ways of God must have been as puzzling to the Jews of that era as they can be to us now.

In fact this story is only round one of a series of encounters between God and Nebuchadnezzar, which ultimately led to his 'conversion', when he was willing to acknowledge the higher kingship of God (by the end of Daniel 4). Here already, God was at work in his mind through dreams with faithful interpretation, showing him his own place in history, where he had got his power from, a true perspective on the empire he was so energetically building, and warning him of the greater power of God himself over all human empires on the earth.

Do we really believe that God can speak in the hearts and minds of unbelievers?

DANIEL AND HIS GOD

When Arioch, the commander of the king's guard, had gone out to put to death the wise men of Babylon, Daniel spoke to him with wisdom and tact. He asked the king's officer, 'Why did the king issue such a harsh decree?' Arioch then explained the

> matter to Daniel. At this, Daniel went in to the king
> and asked for time, so that he might interpret the
> dream for him. *Daniel 2:14–16*

As we meet Daniel again, the first thing that strikes us is that his refusal to compromise over the question of royal food in chapter one did not mean a policy of total non-cooperation with the pagan secular power. He seems only too eager and pleased to help, though presumably the threat of execution concentrated his mind more than a little! On the other hand, he could easily have taken the attitude, 'Interpret your own dream, hated king. If you kill us, we'll be martyrs, but you won't know what your dream meant.' But as we saw in the first chapter, he and his friends had not chosen the path of opting out, of pious separatism, or holy martyrdom. They were now qualified civil servants, busy in the conduct of public administration, but having taken a stand that preserved the distinctiveness and integrity of their faith.

Daniel's prayer fellowship

> Then Daniel returned to his house and explained the
> matter to his friends Hananiah, Mishael and
> Azariah. He urged them to plead for mercy from the
> God of heaven concerning this mystery, so that he
> and his friends might not be executed with the rest
> of the wise men of Babylon. During the night the
> mystery was revealed to Daniel in a vision.
> *Daniel 2:17–19a*

Another chorus we used to sing in our Belfast youth group was:

Dare to be a Daniel, dare to stand alone.

It is true that in a later story Daniel did have to face the lions alone, but in these early chapters we find that he and his friends had continued to provide support and fellowship for one another in their careers. Daniel may have been the spokesman and the one to put his neck on the line by going to the king, but he was not a solitary hero. He asked for and got the prayer support he needed. These young believers worked together. Together they had stuck out their re-education, together they served the state, together they served God. Together they could support each other in keeping their heads — literally and metaphorically. And when they met to pray together, it was not just to escape from their day's work and have some nice cosy fellowship. They brought the pressing problem of their public jobs into the presence of God.

I wish all church fellowship groups did that. So often home groups are mediocre because they float at the level which everybody feels comfortable with and never really engage with the hard realities of the lives of the members. We can escape into intellectual Bible study, or into emotional worship, or even fervent prayer. But we can also leave our real lives with our coats in the hall as we arrive.

One of the best house groups I remember was one where we got down to discussing some moral issues that Christians face today. As we did so, one of the younger members, Alf, who worked at a tyre dealer's, suddenly started talking about all the fiddles and underhand practices that went on at work. Receipts were tampered with; VAT would be charged but not recorded, and then pocketed; stock would disappear. How could he cope with such things, as a junior employee? If he didn't join the rackets, he would stand out like a sore thumb. Worse, he risked hatred and ostracism. On the other hand, if he went to the management, he discovered that they knew perfectly well what was going on, but chose to ignore it to avoid agitation. So if he reported the fiddles, he would be in trouble with both his mates and with the management, and would probably lose his job.

The group suddenly realised that moral issues were no longer just a matter for philosophical discussion, but were an everyday reality for Alf, and put him under considerable pressure and mental stress. We were not able to produce neat solutions to his dilemmas, but we were able to pray for wisdom and strength for him. From then on, the group made sure that people's real problems from work became part of our prayer time regularly. We also got the vicar to arrange preaching and teaching series on Sundays also in which he looked carefully at social and moral issues in the public arena.

In India I used to get invited quite often to speak at seminars of Christian lay people in secular and professional life. I would take them head-first into the sharp-edged Old Testament teaching about integrity, justice, honesty – all the strong ethical heartbeat of Israel's law and prophets – and challenge them as the people of God in today's world to see their mission as being called to live differently from the world around.

Then I would ask them to share the tensions and

problems of living as Christians in India's secular life. It would all come pouring out. The pressure to give or receive bribes (which permeates society from top to bottom), the corruption and dishonest practices, the subtle incentives and not-so-subtle threats, the unscrupulous extortion, the alleged impossibility of being in business at all without participating in the black market on all levels.

On one occasion I asked the group what their churches had to say on such matters and what support they got from their pastors or fellowships. I remember vividly the hollow laughter and sheer amazement that the very idea aroused. 'Our pastors don't preach or teach about such things,' they said. 'Anyway, some of them are no better!' Some of them said that in any case they went to church to *escape* from the wickedness of the world, so they didn't want to hear about it there as well! Whatever the reason, it was clear that there was a gaping chasm between their everyday secular work with all its pressures and problems, and their 'religious' lives. They were getting no support, no prayer, no wrestling together, no applied biblical teaching. No wonder they found it so hard to stand up as Christians and make any effective witness to the light of God's truth in the moral and spiritual darkness of their environment. Daniel could stand before the king alone, because he had knelt before God with his friends.

Daniel's hymn of praise

Then Daniel praised the God of heaven and said:

'Praise be to the name of God for ever and ever;
    wisdom and power are his.
He changes times and seasons;
    he sets up kings and deposes them.
He gives wisdom to the wise
    and knowledge to the discerning.
He reveals deep and hidden things;
    he knows what lies in darkness,
    and light dwells with him.
I thank and praise you, O God of my fathers:
    You have given me wisdom and power,
You have made known to me what we asked of
    you,
    you have made known to us the dream
    of the king.'   *Daniel 2:19b–23*

Not all prayer meetings are perhaps as successful as this one, at least directly. Yet all prayer meetings can follow the example of Daniel's praise here, just as they can learn a lot from a different kind of prayer from his lips in Daniel 9. The prayer focuses on God and his ways, before coming to the personal point at the end. It is always good to start in prayer where Daniel starts here – by affirming great truths about God. This was also how the early church prayed, when they faced an equally life-threatening situation in Acts 4:23–31. Once you have done that, then everything else is put in perspective. Then the truth about God will take priority over our feelings about the situation.

It is important for fellowship groups to learn to do this, otherwise they can become very introverted and sink into a kind of spiritual hypochondria – just look at all our problems, moan, moan. Or they can become little more than a sort of group therapy for the members – a shot of fellowship once a week refreshes the parts other sermons can't reach. But the point of a prayer fellowship is to learn dependence on *God*, not dependence on the fellowship; so God must constantly be exalted and put first. People must know how to affirm his power and ability for themselves, and draw on it when they are on their own again. For even Daniel had to stand alone later when there was no fellowship, as far as we can tell; but his prayer life survived and sustained him when he stared death in the face (Daniel 6).

In his hymn of praise, Daniel affirms two things in particular about God: first, that he controls history (v 21); second, that he reveals his purposes (v 22). Both of these truths are repeatedly demonstrated, in stories and in visions, throughout the rest of the book. God acts and God speaks. He is neither impotent nor silent. Our world doesn't believe that. Even those who like to think they believe in God don't want this kind of God. An opinion poll once asked people if they believed in the God who acts in history. One reply was 'No, just the ordinary one.' Nebuchadnezzar didn't know it, but by asking to have his dream read, he was asking for an encounter with a far from ordinary God. And he was changed by it, eventually. In our Western churches we see so little dynamic change in people and in situations because we have lost the habit of affirming the greatness of God in any meaningful way.

But Daniel also realized that the God he was affirming was also the God who loved to share himself. Notice how the things he says about God are the same things that he claims God has given him: '. . . wisdom and power are his' (v 20) . . . 'You have given me wisdom and power' (v 23). There was no arrogance in this, no blasphemy, simply a statement of fact. Daniel acknowledged that any skill and ability he possessed was his by gift. He admits this to Nebuchadnezzar in verse 30. It took him a long time to persuade Nebuchadnezzar of the same truth in his own case. Jesus promised all the resources of the Holy Spirit to his disciples. He promised that we would do the same (indeed greater) works as he did. Wisdom and strength are there for the asking (James 1:5, 2 Corinthians 12:9, 10).

The source of his ability

> Arioch took Daniel to the king at once and said, 'I have found a man among the exiles from Judah who can tell the king what his dream means.'
>
> The king asked Daniel (also called Belteshazzar), 'Are you able to tell me what I saw in my dream and interpret it?'
>
> Daniel replied, 'No wise man, enchanter, magician or diviner can explain to the king the mystery he has asked about, but there is a God in heaven who reveals mysteries. He has shown King Nebuchadnezzar what will happen in days to come. Your dream and the visions that passed through your mind as you lay on your bed are these. . .'
>
> *Daniel 2:25–28*

There is a British television commercial for the Automobile Association which portrays motorists in various states of distress and incompetence. The crunch question comes up, along the lines of 'Can you fix it?' To

which the desolate answer is 'No', followed by a cheer-
ful, 'But I know a man who can!' Enter the AA man
and all is saved.

Daniel's answer to Nebuchadnezzar is on the same
classic lines. 'Are you able to tell me what I saw . . . ?'
'No! But I know a God who is!' Not, 'Me and my
mates down at the house group have worked it all out
easy.' But, 'There is a God in heaven . . .'

During the 1992 parliamentary election campaign in
Britain I tried to do my little bit to help the Liberal
Democrat party in my local constituency. One evening
I went with our candidate, at the invitation of the staff,
to a residential home for adults with severe learning
difficulties. All kinds of questions were asked and issues
raised, and we did our best to answer them and explain
the differences between the parties. One young lady
had a long list of matters to raise, every one of which
concluded with the question, 'What can we do about
it?' There was the lack of a minibus: 'What can we do
about it?' There were no traffic lights on their road:
'What can we do about it?' There were too few staff;
she didn't like the word 'Disabled' on her bus pass; she
and her friends got insulted on the streets: 'What can
we do about it?' Shirley was most persistent, but it left
the candidate and myself feeling more than somewhat
impotent under the onslaught. We could suggest this
and advise that, but in the end, it was all beyond our
power to do anything very much. We didn't have the
authority or the ability to 'do something about it'. We
would try to persuade those who did, but there was
nothing much else we could 'do about it'.

And as we listen to the speeches of the politicians,
we shrug with a certain scepticism, knowing that their

facility in making promises is not always matched by their ability to fulfil them.

Among the themes and plots of the book of Daniel, there is this ongoing pressure of God on Nebuchadnezzar to force him to see where *real* power and ability are to be found. In this chapter he asks if Daniel is able, and Daniel says only God is. In Daniel 3 he asks Shadrach, Meshach and Abednego if any god will be able to deliver them out of his hand, to which they coolly answer, Yes, their God is able. Nebuchadnezzar finally had to acknowledge that real power lay not in himself, not even in a golden statue of himself, nor in his magicians and all the splendour of his court, nor in his military machine and mighty empire – but with the God of this young Jewish captive, a God he thought he had defeated and captured, but a God who was in reality 'the God of heaven', and very much the God of earth as well. This God, the God of Daniel, is able.

At the end of the chapter, Nebuchadnezzar goes so far as to admit this, within the limited context of the remedy for his nightmare. He can see that God is the source of Daniel's ability. But we can see even more clearly that between the truth that 'God is able', and the fact that 'Daniel was able' (Daniel 2:47), lies the life of prayer and the supportive fellowship that upheld Daniel and his friends in their daily working lives.

GOD AND HIS KINGDOM

At last, after considerable suspense, as in all good story-telling, the reader finds out what this dream was and what it meant.

'You looked, O king, and there before you stood a large statue – an enormous, dazzling statue, awesome in appearance. The head of the statue was made of pure gold, its chest and arms of silver, its belly and thighs of bronze, its legs of iron, its feet partly of iron and partly of baked clay. While you were watching, a rock was cut out, but not by human hands. It struck the statue on its feet of iron and clay and smashed them. Then the iron, the clay, the bronze, the silver and the gold were broken to pieces at the same time and became like chaff on a threshing-floor in the summer. The wind swept them away without leaving a trace. But the rock that struck the statue became a huge mountain and filled the whole earth.'
Daniel 2:31–35

Nebuchadnezzar's dream was weird: a great statue, a mixture of great glory and crazy instability, full of inner contradictions by being made partly of costly and useful metals, but partly of a stupid and impossible mixture of metal and pottery. And this weakest part was at the place where it most needed to be strongest – at the bottom; all that gleaming glory, but on a fragile, crumbling base.

And then came the rock, a rock that he somehow knew in his dream had not been quarried by mere mortals. So where had it come from? And as it smashed into the feet of clay, the whole statue collapsed; but it didn't just fall, it crumbled to dust and was blown away in the wind, like the corpse of Dracula at the end of the film. The rock, however, like some living monster, grew ever bigger till it filled the earth. This is the stuff that science fiction movies are made of.

No wonder Nebuchadnezzar was troubled. If the

dream was about him, then which part was he supposed to play? Perhaps the statue meant his enemies, and he would be the rock who would smash them all and take over worldwide power. But supposing the statue were his own empire! Was it really so fragile? Were his people such an impossible mixture of races that they would end up falling apart? And who or what was this smashing, pulverizing rock? Was some unknown enemy lurking on his borders?

Daniel then moves on to interpret the dream for Nebuchadnezzar, to his relief and the readers' as well.

> 'This was the dream, and now we will interpret it to the king. You, O king, are the king of kings. The God of heaven has given you dominion and power and might and glory; in your hands he has placed mankind and the beasts of the field and the birds of the air. Wherever they live, he has made you ruler over them all. You are that head of gold.
>
> 'After you, another kingdom will rise, inferior to yours. Next, a third kingdom, one of bronze, will rule over the whole earth. Finally, there will be a fourth kingdom, strong as iron — for iron breaks and smashes everything — and as iron breaks things to pieces, so it will crush and break all the others. Just as you saw that the feet and toes were partly of baked clay and partly of iron, so this will be a divided kingdom; yet it will have some of the strength of iron in it, even as you saw iron mixed with clay. As the toes were partly iron and partly clay, so this kingdom will be partly strong and partly brittle. And just as you saw the iron mixed with baked clay, so the people will be a mixture and will not remain united, any more than iron mixes with clay.

'In the time of those kings, the God of heaven will set up a kingdom that will never be destroyed, nor will it be left to another people. It will crush all those kingdoms and bring them to an end, but it will itself endure for ever. This is the meaning of the vision of the rock cut out of a mountain, but not by human hands – a rock that broke the iron, the bronze, the clay, the silver and the gold to pieces.

'The great God has shown the king what will take place in the future. The dream is true and the interpretation is trustworthy.'   *Daniel 2:36–45*

Daniel's interpretation is nothing less than a theology of history. It is not, however, a *timetable* for history. People get bogged down trying to identify and date all the parts of his interpretation, which the text does not do, and then miss its real significance.

Daniel starts in the present and then moves on to the future. In the present, he states a matter of fact, and then gives a theological interpretation of it. 'You, O king,' he says to Nebuchadnezzar, 'are the king of kings.' To us who are used to this as an expression of praise to God, this sounds a bit over the top, but it was a simple fact. Nebuchadnezzar was the great king over a number of smaller states whose kings had been forced into submission to him, Israel's own king being one of them. So Daniel begins at the top of the dream statue and affirms that Nebuchadnezzar himself was the head of gold. No flattering, just current reality.

But then Daniel adds his theological insight. All this golden glitter, power and glory belonged to Nebuchadnezzar *only because the God of heaven had given it to him*. Nebuchadnezzar was Top Man of the Top

Nation by divine permission and appointment. Now, Nebuchadnezzar probably already believed this in a kind of way. Ancient kings tended to attribute their power to their gods, since it bolstered their reign by giving it an air of divine approval. But there is no doubt that Daniel himself, when he used the expression 'the God of heaven', meant by it Yahweh, *his* God, the God of his people, and the only true and living God. The God of Israel had given supreme power to the king of Babylon! That must have sounded richly ironic, given the position of the two peoples – Israel in captivity and Babylon in power!

Exactly the same understanding of contemporary history was expressed by Jeremiah, when he gatecrashed a diplomatic conference in Jerusalem at which all the ambassadors of the small states around Judah had met to plan rebellion against Nebuchadnezzar. Wearing a yoke around his neck as a symbolic gesture, he told all those foreign diplomats that Yahweh the God of Israel had given authority to Nebuchadnezzar, and the only safe course was for all their countries to submit to him.

> 'With my great power and outstretched arm I [God] made the earth and its people and the animals that are on it, and I give it to anyone I please. Now I will hand all your countries over to my servant Nebuchadnezzar king of Babylon; I will make even the wild animals subject to him.'
>
> *Jeremiah 27:5, 6*

'*Nebuchadnezzar my servant*'! The very idea seems outrageous. But this was how Jeremiah and Daniel interpreted the events they were living through. It called for a great depth of faith and a broad view of God's sovereignty to do so. Think of the tragic events they were submerged in. Think of the national hatred of a figure like Nebuchadnezzar. Think of the unpopularity of anyone who could stand up and call him Yahweh's servant, or a 'head of gold'. But God's control of history and the mystery of his plans are wider than our prejudices.

For a generation since the end of the Second World War, we in the West were taught to believe that the world was divided into two. There was the 'free world' and there was 'the Soviet bloc' (the Third World was invented later). We knew whose side the angels were on. We were told that everything east of the Iron Curtain was 'the evil empire'. Whose side was God on? The answer seemed so obvious and numerous apocalyptic scenarios, in books, comics and films, portrayed the final great battle of Armageddon being fought with the legions of communism all on one side against the forces of (self-) righteousness on the other.

Writing on this side of 1990, it seems hard to believe and to remember all that after the revolutionary changes which swept through Europe in 1989–90. If we see the hand of God in it (as Christians of central and eastern Europe certainly do) then we equally have to acknowledge that the human trigger was Mikhail Gorbachev, President of the former Soviet Union. God did not use any of the leaders of the so-called 'Christian' West – though some of them like to claim that we 'won the Cold War'.

Yet where is Gorbachev now? Not only is he no longer a president, but the state of which he was president no longer exists! There is a divine irony, sense of humour almost, that the grip of communist tyranny in

Europe should be smashed, not by the might of its enemies, but by the policies of its foremost head of state. 'God moves in mysterious ways.' He raises up human leaders, gives them temporary ability and power to set in motion processes and events which achieve his purpose, and when they have fulfilled that role, he sets them down and moves on. Nobody is indispensable.

Daniel then moves on to give a general outline of the scheme of history to follow, based on the succession of metals. He says these represent a succession of kings to follow Nebuchadnezzar. No identification is given and we need not pause at this point to try to name names. The main points in what Daniel says are the following.

• *The power of the fourth kingdom*. It will be enormously powerful, but will have an inherent disunity and instability because of its divided nature.

• *The fall of the statue*. This will be partly because of its own intrinsic fragility and instability. There is here a picture of the ultimate failure of all human power and arrogant claims. In the end all that human beings so proudly build, 'tower and temple fall to dust'. This picture of a series of governments coming to an end with the fall of the most powerful one could be illustrated from many periods of human history, including our own generation. In this century we have had a 'Thousand Year Reich', and a Berlin Wall whose builder announced would last a thousand years – just months before it was demolished. Another prophet put it like this:

He brings princes to naught and reduces the rulers
   of this world to nothing.
No sooner are they planted,
  no sooner are they sown,
  no sooner do they take root in the ground,
than he blows on them and they wither,
   and a whirlwind sweeps them away like chaff.

Isaiah 40: 23, 24

● *The arrival of the rock.* The fall of the statue was not just because it had feet of clay, but because it was struck and destroyed by the rock not cut by human hands. The statue crumbles but the rock remains, and in Daniel's interpretation, this rock stands for the kingdom of God himself which will ultimately replace all human kingdoms. Although he describes it only briefly, his words are powerfully prophetic of a number of aspects of the kingdom of God as we find it in the Gospels.

It comes from outside. That is, this kingdom is not just one of the series of human kingdoms. It has its origin elsewhere. This is what Jesus meant when he said, 'My kingdom is not *of* this world'. He did not mean it was purely spiritual or that it had nothing to do with political power. He meant it had its origin and source not from human power, but from God's power.

It is established in the earth. It replaces the other kingdoms, but not the earth itself. The kingdom of God is not just an escape to heaven, but the establishing of the rule of God over the earth itself.

It is the work of God, and is therefore indestructible. It will bring all human kingdoms to an end, but will itself endure forever.

It will grow and spread. There will be a process of its

establishment, until eventually it will fill the whole earth. Jesus made the same point in many of his parables about the kingdom of God (eg the mustard seed, yeast in the dough, a net in the sea, etc).

So Daniel gave this pagan king a theology lesson. His own personal power was a grant from the living God, but it would not last forever. The future held a succession of human kingdoms, but the future ultimately belongs to the kingdom of God.

For Nebuchadnezzar, the dream and its interpretation were meant to bring him face to face with the spiritual realities that lie behind the externals of history. He should see his own political power in the light of its transience. Neither he nor his empire were going to last forever. Heads of gold have a precarious future if they rest on feet of clay, but there is a higher king and a more permanent kingdom. The question was, would he acknowledge them? To a limited extent, yes, he did.

> Then king Nebuchadnezzar fell prostrate before Daniel and paid him honour and ordered that an offering and incense be presented to him. The king said to Daniel, 'Surely your God is the God of gods and the Lord of kings and a revealer of mysteries, for you were able to reveal this mystery.'
>
> *Daniel 2:46, 47*

However, one gets the impression that this was not so much the act of a man sobered by an encounter with God as the relief of a man who thinks his own power is not immediately threatened.

For Daniel and his friends, and for all those in their situation – believers caught in a hostile empire – it was a reassurance that their God was still on the throne. Their lifetime might be lived out under the thumb of a Nebuchadnezzar, not to mention his metallic successors, but in the end the future was secure because it lay with God and the rock of his kingdom.

And it is this same reassurance that Daniel 2 gives to Christians caught in the pressures of living in the midst of a pagan environment, where so much seems to be weighted in favour of the powers of this world with all their pomp and glory, their evil and corruption. For what Daniel saw only as a vision for the future is now a present reality at work in the world. The reign of God has begun through the coming of Christ and in his death and resurrection. One day it will be established in all its fullness when Christ returns to claim his kingdom. Then 'the earth will be filled with the knowledge of God as the waters cover the sea.' Until then 'God is working his purpose out as year succeeds to year', and every act of obedience, every word of witness, every courageous stand for the truth, is worthwhile and vindicated in the light of that future.

It is in this light that we must read the last few verses of this chapter.

> Then the king placed Daniel in a high position and lavished many gifts on him. He made him ruler over the entire province of Babylon and placed him in charge of all its wise men. Moreover, at Daniel's request the king appointed Shadrach, Meshach and Abednego administators over the province of Babylon, while Daniel himself remained at the royal court. *Daniel 2:48, 49*

The point is not merely that Daniel and his friends got

promotion, but also that they continued in the political civil service of a king they now knew to be a head of gold on feet of clay. They went back to work. They turned up at the office next Monday. They did not set up a community of spiritual hope to await the arrival of the rock. Whether or not they were able to continue to meet for their prayer fellowship we cannot tell. But certainly the strength they had derived from it enabled them to face an even tougher test in the future.

So we conclude by noting again the importance of integrating our working lives as Christians with our spiritual fellowship and prayer, and holding on to God's call to both. Daniel and his friends probably experienced more revelations and visions from God than an average Christian home group is likely to get in a lifetime. Yet the effect was not to stick their heads in clouds of piety, nor even to set them up in glossy 'prophetic' ministries. They didn't even go off to Bible college to develop their new found spiritual gifts. They got on with the job they had trained for. They stuck to their desks. And God used Shadrach, Meshach and Abednego (Daniel 3), and Daniel (Daniel 4), to far greater effect in their impact on the king than if they had thundered like Amos or blazed like Elijah.

3
BOW
OR
BURN

My daughter got a job for a while as a kitchen porter, the lowest of the low in the ranks of the catering trade, in a fair-sized hotel. Thrown in with quite an assortment of local humanity, she actually thrived on the hurly-burly of social chit-chat and arguments in the work-place. 'It's really good when people get to know you're a Christian,' she once said to me, 'because it makes the conversation far more controversial!'

Well, that's fine! But it's one thing to enjoy a good barney over the stove in a context where the fact that you have some peculiar beliefs and opinions brightens the day for everybody. It's something very different if those convictions throw you into serious conflict in which your job itself and many other important things in life could be threatened.

It's all very well to take a stand for your faith when

you are a young student, perhaps, like Daniel and his friends had been when they first arrived in Babylon. Then it's almost the done thing to be filled with idealism and system-bucking heroism, with the added luxury of being free from the responsibilities of family and career. You may risk some popularity but not much more.

Later in life, the realities of the world of business can squeeze a person's faith much more severely. How can you live in the real world unless you go along with its ways? It's not so much a matter of bowing to idols as bowing to the inevitable, surely. The world can demand a high price from those who refuse to do things its way.

Here we find Daniel's friends, who had quietly stood with him in their act of conscientious objection to one feature of their re-education by the Babylonian state, now facing a much more threatening test of loyalty to their faith.

The least that Daniel had done for Nebuchadnezzar so far was to cure his bad dreams. What he had actually tried to do was to confront him with the God who controls history and the future, and make him face up to his own place in the scheme of things. He was the head of a great empire, but there was a kingdom greater than his and, in the end, it would be God's kingdom that would stand the test of time when 'the rock' had reduced all human empires to rubble. But Nebuchadnezzar was not ready to face anything like that – yet. It would have put his present status and power at the head of the greatest world empire in question. It would have debunked some of his golden dreams. By the end of Daniel 4 we shall find a very different Nebuchadnezzar singing a very different tune. But for the moment, his agenda centred on his own plans.

Freed from the disturbance of his recurring nightmare, he set about solving the problem it represented. If the statue was unstable because of its fragile feet, Nebuchadnezzar decided to strengthen its golden head – himself and his young state. The shattering rock outside human control could be forgotten. If his empire had weaknesses caused by disunity, then he must create a united, harmonious people bound together by ties of political loyalty, religious zeal and cultural pride. It was this decision and the policy it led to that caused problems for Daniel's friends, and doubtless other Jewish believers.

The issue now facing them was one which believers, Jewish and Christian, have wrestled with all down the ages. What are the limits of patriotism? How is it possible, on the one hand, to obey instructions such as Jeremiah 29:7 and Romans 13:1–7 to seek the good of the country where God has put you, showing loyal submission and good citizenship, and on the other hand to remain faithful to God's command to worship him alone? Is loyalty to one's own culture and country a good thing? When does it become actually idolatrous, that is, taking that place of ultimate importance that should belong only to God? Can we refuse to obey the state authorities and, if so, for what reasons? And can we expect God always to bail us out if we do? These can be hard enough questions for believers who are ordinary citizens. For those who hold public office, in political life or in civil administration for the government, it can sometimes be a dilemma of literally life and death proportions.

THE CLAIMS OF THE STATE

> King Nebuchadnezzar made an image of gold, ninety feet high and nine feet wide, and set it up on the plain of Dura in the province of Babylon. He then summoned the satraps, prefects, governors, advisors, treasurers, judges, magistrates and all the other provincial officials to come to the dedication of the image he had set up. So the satraps, prefects, governors, advisers, treasurers, judges, magistrates and all the other provincial officials assembled for the dedication of the image that King Nebuchadnezzar had set up, and they stood before it.
>
> Then the herald loudly proclaimed, 'This is what you are commanded to do, O peoples, nations and men of every language: As soon as you hear the sound of the horn, flute, zither, lyre, harp, pipes and all kinds of music, you must fall down and worship the image of gold that King Nebuchadnezzar has set up. Whoever does not fall down and worship will immediately be thrown into a blazing furnace.'
>
> Therefore, as soon as they heard the sound of the horn, flute, zither, lyre, harp and all kinds of music, all the peoples, nations and men of every language fell down and worshipped the image of gold that King Nebuchadnezzar had set up.
>
> *Daniel 3:1–7*

'The image of gold which Nebuchadnezzar set up.' This phrase echoes throughout Daniel 3. The statue itself is very much centre stage in the whole drama. It is unmistakably meant to remind the reader or listener of the head of gold in Nebuchadnezzar's dream statue in the last chapter. We are not told exactly what this golden statue was an image of. Probably it was not any of the gods of Babylon, because they are distinguished from it in verse 12. So it may have been a stylized image of Nebuchadnezzar himself, or of his imperial power. It may have been a huge monument to the Babylonian empire itself – 'The Spirit of Babylon'. It was certainly enormous, thirty metres tall, and three metres at the base, a gleaming, thrusting shaft of imperial glory and state power.

What was it for? It was not merely a token of Nebuchadnezzar's personal pride, though that was great enough. Rather it was intended as a symbol of the unity and strength of the empire. We know from Daniel 1 that Babylon ruled over a great mixture of nations and peoples who are referred to in this chapter as 'peoples, nations and men of every language' (vs 4, 7). Nebuchadnezzar's plan was to produce some kind of political unity by imposing a sacred ideology of the state itself – a national religion and culture – for official purposes. He would harness religious zeal and cultural pride (notice the emphasis on all kinds of music) – a very powerful combination in any age. There would be no prohibition of the worship of other gods, of course. People could keep and worship the gods of their own nations and cultures, so long as they gave priority to the official state gods of Babylon. One king, one empire, one official faith.

And he arranged a massive 'Festival of Babylon' around the golden statue that symbolized it all. It would be a great unifying spectacular, both enabling and enforcing the kind of imperial loyalty and devotion that he needed to stabilize and strengthen his relatively young empire. It was an exercise in nation-building. Let everybody publicly declare their allegiance to him, the great benefactor and father of the nation. Let all the ethnic groups in his realms keep their own culture, but let it be subordinated to the common endeavour. Perhaps he arranged that all the musical traditions of the different groups would take it in turns to display their heritage, so long as it was done in honour of his golden statue. That way he would allow for the expression of regional differences and local pride, but harness it all to his desired imperial unity. National unity, national security, national pride – these were the powerful driving forces behind Nebuchadnezzar's great, gleaming, golden festival.

So Nebuchadnezzar's state staked its claim to total allegiance and called on every loyal citizen to acknowledge it. And they did, as people still do when the drums and music of national pride begin to beat. From the top to the bottom of society they turn out to celebrate. There is intentional humour in the repeated lists of officials and of musical instruments. Everybody who was anybody was there. It was the place to be seen. It was noisy, it was festive, it was mesmerising, it was infectious. It was Nebuchadnezzar's Babylon. And such is the seductive power of such great, state-sponsored celebrations that most people were probably there quite willingly, gratefully even. However, just in case, there was always the 'burning fiery furnace' in the background. Not that it would ever be needed, of course, but state policies need state sanctions, and people should realize that the government is serious. 'Bow or burn! Toast the king or toast yourself!' Nobody in their right mind would quarrel, surely.

Such, then, was the claim of Nebuchadnezzar's

state. It was basically the same as what has come to be known as 'totalitarianism' – ie, the view that the state itself is the ultimate reality which governs the totality of the lives of its subjects and demands complete loyalty and obedience. It is a claim that has been echoed and repeated many times down through the centuries, right into our own. Nebuchadnezzar was not the first or the last to link patriotism, religion and culture for the political benefit of the state itself. In how many countries, ancient and modern, western and non-western, have we seen this combination? The state claims total allegiance and justifies it on grounds of necessity, for stability, for ethnic survival, for higher ideals even. And when the state begins to make such claims, it leaves no alternative except the fire, or its many equivalents.

The state is a human institution which seems to have a built-in tendency towards idolatry, to claim divine authority and demand total allegiance. This tendency flows from our fallen human insecurity. Having rejected God as the source of authority and security, we long for anything that will give life order, stability, security, regularity and social glue. When a powerful state promises these things, we are prepared to pay a high price to buy it. Or perhaps, more accurately, when the crunch comes, we are not prepared to pay the higher price of not buying it.

Western Christians are rightly grateful for the freedom we currently enjoy from such blatant totalitarianism. We are also acutely conscious still of the high price that was indeed paid to remove just such a virulent tyranny in Europe. Christians in central and eastern Europe have lived for two generations with the shackles of such a state ideology, and now rejoice to have lived to see them loosed. More thoughtful Christians among them, however, wonder if they may have exchanged the ideology of Marxist materialism for the worship of Western capitalist materialism. Both can be blatantly idolatrous, and neither has any place for the living God.

But there are many other parts of the world where Christians live under regimes that demand loyalty to other gods, whether they be the remaining communist states in South East Asia and China, or the increasing number of countries, such as Pakistan and Malaysia, where Islamic government is reducing or removing the religious and civil rights of adherents of other faiths. Even in a country such as India, which is constitutionally secular, the weight of Hinduism is so great in every fibre of public and community life that it can be a very costly thing to preserve a distinctive Christian identity or allegiance in some places. The goals of some Hindu nationalist movements is certainly to achieve the sort of unity of religion, nationality and culture that Nebuchadnezzar sought. There is, they argue, only one religion for the patriotic Indian. Any other religious allegiance is deemed essentially traitorous. Indian Christians are told that they cannot be true Indians with such a Western religion, in spite of the fact that Christianity is easily one of the oldest religions in India, certainly older than Islam or Sikhism, and arrived there long before the conversion of 'the west' (ie, pagan Europe) to Christianity was complete.

THE COST OF MONOTHEISM

At this time some astrologers came forward and denounced the Jews. They said to King Nebuchadnezzar, 'O king, live for ever! You have issued a decree, O king, that everyone who hears the sound of the horn, flute, zither, lyre, harp, pipes and all kinds of music must fall down and worship the image of gold, and that whoever does not fall down and worship will be thrown into a blazing furnace. But there are some Jews whom you have set over the affairs of the province of Babylon – Shadrach, Meshach and Abednego – who pay no attention to you, O king. They neither serve your gods nor worship the image of gold you have set up.'

Furious with rage, Nebuchadnezzar summoned Shadrach, Meshach and Abednego. So these men were brought before the king, and Nebuchadnezzar said to them, 'Is it true, Shadrach, Meshach and Abednego, that you do not serve my gods or worship the image of gold I have set up? Now when you hear the sound of the horn, flute, zither, lyre, harp, pipes and all kinds of music, if you are ready to fall down and worship the image I made, very good. But if you do not worship it, you will be thrown immediately into a blazing furnace. Then what god will be able to rescue you from my hand?'

Daniel 3:8–15

The issue came to a crunch for Shadrach, Meshach and Abednego, though probably not at their own instigation. Rather we get the impression that this sudden conflict between them and the state government was, first of all, *uninvited*. Their whole demeanour and comments when they are brought before the king suggests that they had in fact tried to avoid such a confrontation. Perhaps they had just stayed away from the festival. At any rate, there is nothing in the text which justifies the Sunday school flannelgraph pictures I remember as a child in which one saw a whole plain full of millions of people, all bowed face to the ground like Muslims at prayer, except for these three men proudly standing to attention in the middle. It seems far more likely that they did not adopt such a deliberate posture of defiance, but simply chose not to participate, which would fit better with their policy as seen earlier in chapter one. There we observed their polite refusal to accept one particular detail of their training, against a background of remarkable cultural acceptance and adaptation on other issues. These men were not martyrdom hunters, looking for any opportunity to parade their religious affiliation, keen for a confrontation with the authorities. They were conscientious civil servants getting on with their daily work.

Secondly, we get the impression, having read through the book thus far, that this sudden test of their faithfulness to God was *unexpected*. Surely, they must have thought, they had got this thing sorted out right at the beginning of their career in government office. They had taken a stand then and it had been accepted. After that they had got on with the job they were trained for and, as far as we know, they had faced no further serious problem of conscience. Their Babylonian government service had not involved any compromise of their faith commitment to their God. Yet now, suddenly, they are hurled into a conflict with the king himself. Not only was it sudden and unexpected, it was also terrifyingly threatening – one minute a respectable and responsible job in high office, next minute facing the flames of instant execution.

Believers can never afford to relax. The tide of human politics can turn amazingly fast, whether for good or ill. The Israelites were comfortable in Egypt until 'there arose a Pharaoh who did not know about Joseph' and suddenly their privileged guest status became one of intolerable exploitation. David was court musician one day and dodging javelins the next. Elijah was a public hero on Mount Carmel one day and running for his life from Jezebel the next. The crowds who flocked around Jesus one week to cheer him on his way were calling for his death within a few days. And so it has been through history. States which in one era have welcomed Christian missionaries have sometimes turned to fierce persecution. America, a land founded by people escaping from religious intolerance has lately spawned the unimaginably intolerant 'Politically Correct' phenomenon. In Britain, it is not inconceivable that laws designed originally to penalise racial hatred and inflammatory words and actions, could be turned against any form of evangelism among communities of other faiths.

We need to remember that we live in a world which, as a whole, is in rebellion against God. So if it happens that for the present we live in comfort or under a benevolent regime, it is likely to prove a transient interlude in the great sweep of human history rather than a permanent state of affairs. 'Beware when all men speak well of you,' said Jesus. The word of denunciation and the threat of the fiery furnace may be just around the corner.

However, for our three friends, the way things turn out now vindicates and shows up the importance of the stand they took earlier. Then they had stood firm over what may have seemed a small issue. They had refused to enter into the kind of covenant table fellowship with the king that would have symbolized total allegiance and dependence. Way back then, in the early days of their captivity and of Nebuchadnezzar's reign, it may have seemed very remote indeed that Nebuchadnezzar would ever make such an absolute claim. At the time his policy seemed to have been to give relative encouragement to the different ethnic and religious groups in his empire – apart from the fact, of course, that they were conquered and their gods were subservient to his. The totalitarian claim of absolute allegiance, and what amounted to worship of the state itself, was not then required of them, or at least they were able to duck out of it.

But now that absolute, blasphemous claim was standing ninety feet high in the blue sky and they could not avoid it. And even if they tried to lie low, their refusal was noticed by others and professional jealousy soon did its work, as it later does again in Daniel 6. However, it was their earlier decision which strengthened this one. In their student days they had set the direction and the limits of their commitment in a relatively small matter. Now that decision was tested by fire when the issue was far greater. 'He that is faithful in small things can be trusted to be faithful in great things.'

Thirdly, we can reflect on how *tempting* the situation was for them. They were not, after all, being called upon explicitly to deny Yahweh their God, at least not in the eyes of the king and his polytheistic contemporaries. It was just a matter of a quick bow to Nebuchadnezzar and his statue. 'Why insist on your monotheism at such a cost? Nobody is asking you to deny your own God – just accept the national symbols for the common good.' The argument has a very subtle persuasive force. It points up the utter contrast between true monotheism and all forms of polytheism, between biblical faith and religious pluralism.

The seduction of polytheism is that it appears to widen every choice and set no limits. It can tolerate anything – except, of course, the person who insists that there is only one true God. Then tolerance can lead to fiery furnaces. In India, the vast ocean of Hindu polytheism seems to allow for anything and to pervade everything. Because there is only one final reality, then all religious ways are deemed to lead to it in the end. So everything is tolerated *except* the view that there is only one way. Strictly biblical monotheism, and especially the conviction of the uniqueness of Christ as saviour, are frowned upon.

It is thus very hard for many ordinary Christians to be truly and consistently monotheistic in practice as well as confession. The temptations and demands of the surrounding polytheism, seemingly harmless and socially expected, are part of everyday life. It is very hard to distinguish between what is 'cultural' and what is 'religious', since they are so closely intertwined and mutually reinforcing. Christians who take a stand for their monotheism and refuse to take part in activities such as dedications to Hindu deities in the work place, or neighbourhood collections for Hindu festivals, can find themselves facing ostracism, dismissal, violence to themselves or their homes, discrimination against their children, even death threats. Loyalty to Christ alone can be costly, personally and socially. Far easier to keep your monotheism in your heart and keep society happy with passing nods to the gods when required.

Doubtless that was how Nebuchadnezzar tried to

reason with his three government officers. There would have been the man to man approach. 'Let's not make a big fuss over this. Why be so narrow? After all, I am your king – the one who you claim was actually appointed by your own God! So surely even your God will expect you to demonstrate your loyalty to me and my state. Why waste your lives for a futile gesture of religious intolerance?'

But they would not give in, and prepared themselves to face the cost of the central, revealed truth of their faith. Yahweh is God and there is no other.

THE COURAGE OF FAITH

> Shadrach, Meshach and Abednego replied to the king, 'O Nebuchadnezzar, we do not need to defend ourselves before you in this matter. If we are thrown into the blazing furnace, the God we serve is able to save us from it, and he will rescue us from your hand, O king. But even if he does not, we want you to know, O king, that we will not serve your gods or worship the image of gold you have set up.'
>
> *Daniel 3:16–18*

These are staggeringly impressive verses. The reply of the three friends to Nebuchadnezzar is dignified and confident, full of trust in God and yet not presumptuous before him. The first thing to note is how they coolly deflate the king's arrogance. Look at the contrast between what he says at the end of verse 15 and the way they answer in verse 16.

'What god can deliver you from my hand?' he asks,

as if to say, 'I, Nebuchadnezzar, am better than the average god.' It was a not too subtly disguised claim to divinity. Or at least it was an assertion that, as far as the present issue was concerned, his actual royal power mattered far more than any religious faith.

Part of Nebuchadnezzar's problem, as Daniel 4 shows clearly, was that he was quite happy for the gods to rule in heaven, just so long as it was clear who ruled on earth. With his fiery furnace round the corner, it must have seemed a perfectly reasonable assumption to make. Anyhow, that is how he addresses these three mere civil servants. What madness to imagine that their absurdly narrow religious scruples would be any match for his absolute power!

But Shadrach, Meshach and Abednego simply reply, 'Listen, Nebuchadnezzar . . .' They use his simple name. No titles, no honorifics, no optimistic 'O king, live for ever'. They address him as a man, nothing more. He might have a ninety foot statue beside him, but under all his robes and gold plate, and in spite of all his absurd claims, he was just plain Nebuchadnezzar. He was their king, yes; but a man like them.

Furthermore, they refuse to grovel or excuse them-selves. Their record speaks for itself. 'We have no need to defend ourselves in this matter.' They had served the king competently and with integrity, and their religious affiliation had never stood in the way of that before.

Then they go on to an even more courageous bit of mimicry. They turn the king's threats head over heels. 'If you will bow,' he had said, 'then well and good . . . but if not, then . . .' (v 15). 'If you throw us in the fire,' they replied, 'then . . . but even if not . . .' (v 17).

It was cool. It was courageous. But really it was

nothing more than the facts as they saw them. 'You do what you like, Nebuchadnezzar. Either way, we can't meet your demands.' But alongside this coolness, there was also a remarkable confidence in God, expressed in classic terms in verse 17. Every phrase counts.

• '*The God . . .*' Who was that? Yahweh, the God of Israel, the God of all their history, Yahweh of the exodus, Yahweh of Sinai, Yahweh of the conquest. These Jewish believers, with their first class degrees in the literature, philosophy, arts and science of Babylon, had not forgotten their childhood faith. They were still part of that covenant people of God, who could call God 'our God' and draw infinite resources of strength and courage from the possessive pronoun alone.

• ' . . . *we serve . . .*' They say this as they stand in front of their political lord and master. 'Yes, Nebuchadnezzar, we are your civil servants, and good ones too. But in serving you we actually serve our God who appointed you.' They did not quite say, as another more famous Jew said when he too stood before a hostile political power on trial for his life, 'You would have no power over us unless it was permitted you by God', but that was certainly what they meant.

• ' . . . *is able to save us from [the fire] . . .*' Of course he is! Who made fire in the first place? The same God who made the sea and then rescued Israel from it. The omnipotence of Yahweh was a proven part of every Jew's creed. As we have already seen in chapter two, there is a little sub-plot running through Daniel as to who really 'is able'. Where does the real executive ability in world affairs lie? Civil servants don't always know the answer to that question, but these three did.

• '... *and he will rescue us from your hand, O king.*' As an Ulsterman might say, 'Catch yourself on, Nebuchadnezzar. If it's a fight you're wanting, then you and your swanky image are no match for our God.' It is the simplicity of their reply that is so impressive. We have to pad it out to get its full flavour, but its simplicity is majestic. There's no argument at all, just a quiet confidence in God's ability to save.

Verse 18, however, is even more arresting:

• '*But even if he does not ...* ' These are the crucial words in their reply to the king. They should not be taken as a sudden lapse into doubt and uncertainty. It's not a case of hedging bets and covering all options. Rather it is a triumphant affirmation of complete faith in God which still leaves God his freedom to do as he pleases. They fully expected a miracle, but they would serve God without one. They declared total faith in God's ability, along with the total acceptance of God's freedom.

This is a combination which is not easy to hold together in practical everyday life, let alone in life threatening tests of faith. It sounds rather contrary to some kinds of popular teaching today on the sure-fire certainty of faith. Certainly it doesn't fit easily with the insurance policy kind of faith – 'Name it and claim it'. We are told that any need we may have which requires a dash of the miraculous should be ours if we claim it by faith. 'Never say, "If it be your will", when praying for something, especially when praying for healing', I was once told. 'God is able and God always will.' Verse 17 alone could lead us to think that way, if it were not for verse 18 immediately after. 'God is still God, and he may choose to let us fry. But even if he does, we affirm our faith in him and will not serve your gods' (not that they would have been in any fit state to do so, but this was not the moment for logical niceties).

I remember an African student who arrived one Sunday in our fellowship meeting in Pune, India. What a testimony she had! She was not really qualified to have got admission to the university, but she believed it was where God wanted her, so she claimed it . . . and got it. She had no ticket for her flight, but she claimed it . . . and got it. And so it went on, one thing after another for which she had trusted God and he had come up trumps every time. It was stirring stuff and we all rejoiced with her and praised God. I don't think I am a cynical person, and I did not for a moment doubt her word or sincerity. But I couldn't help wondering how her faith would cope with the first time God says 'No' to her, for he undoubtedly will (or has already, I expect). It is a great relief to me to know that God's wisdom is greater than mine, and that I can trust him to say no if my requests are way off beam. He can do miracles for any of us, but I am glad he is not bound to our every notion. Even our sincerest requests may need to be overridden by his wise refusal.

More seriously, even the Bible shows that God can rescue some but allow others to suffer or die, without explanation. Have you ever wondered how John, the brother of James, felt when Peter had his miraculous, angelic, rescue from prison, whereas James had been executed by Herod only shortly before (Acts 12)? Did the church not pray for James? Did James not pray for himself? One presumes so, but God said no. A sword for James, an angel for Peter. Why save Peter and let

James die? Only God knows the answer.

And even that most famous chapter which describes the heroes of faith and what God accomplished through them, Hebrews 11, reminds us that all was not glory and miracles. Hebrews 11:33–35a is an amplification of Daniel 3:17.

> [Those] who through faith conquered kingdoms, administered justice, and gained what was promised; who shut the mouths of lions, quenched the fury of the flames, and escaped the edge of the sword; whose weakness was turned to strength; and who became powerful in battle and routed foreign armies. Women received back their dead, raised to life again.

Hebrews 11:35b–38 is more like Daniel 3:18.

> Others were tortured and refused to be released, so that they might gain a better resurrection. Some faced jeers and flogging, while still others were chained and put in prison. They were stoned; they were sawn in two; they were put to death by the sword. They went about in sheepskins and goatskins, destitute, persecuted and mistreated – the world was not worthy of them. They wandered in deserts and mountains, and in caves and holes in the ground.

The great encouragement of those verses in Hebrews 11 is that, whether you end up among the 'some' who mixed it with miracles, or the 'others' who were killed, 'these were *all* commended for their faith' (v 39). In other words, when someone we know (or ourselves, for that matter) seems to be left in the lurch in spite of prayer and whatever other ministry is done for them, when a friend is not healed, when the miracle doesn't happen, when the persecution or suffering just goes on, we should not jump to the conclusion that they did not have faith, or enough faith. To think or say that is usually untrue and pastorally disastrous.

Coming back to our three friends, we find the real basis of their ability to live with the 'but if not' is in their double affirmation: 'The God we serve . . . we will not serve your gods'. In other words, 'we do not serve our God just because he is stronger than your gods, though he is. Nor do we serve him just because he can work miracles for us, though he can. We serve him ultimately because he is in fact the only God around to be served. He is the only Lord, alone worthy to be served, worshipped and obeyed. It is not a choice between serving our God or serving your gods. That is a choice open only to a polytheist. It is merely a choice between serving or not serving the *only* true and living God. And we choose to serve him, whatever he chooses to do regarding us.'

Now that is the mark of real faith. It is the determination to go on serving and trusting God in the face of any 'if not . . .' It is being able to say, 'Lord, I believe that you are able to protect me and my family from all danger, illness, accident or death. But even if not, I will not bow down and serve the god of bitterness.'

'I believe you are able to preserve my reputation, and my job, if I take a stand for what I believe to be right and just. But even if not, even if I lose all of that, I will not bow down and serve the god of cowardice and go the way of the world.'

'I believe you are able to open the door into that job, that ministry, that country, that opportunity that seems so right to me. But even if not, and I seem to be walking in the dark, I will not bow down and serve the gods of despair and anxiety.'

'I believe you are able to help me find a life partner and enjoy all your normal gifts of marriage and family. But even if not, I will not bow down and serve the gods of self-pity.'

Do not be afraid of the 'if not . . .'. It is not doubt or unbelief. It is the humble acceptance of God's sovereign freedom to do with us as he will, and to put us to the ultimate test of faithfulness if he chooses. Then, as the disciples did, we should pray for the grace to count it an honour to suffer for his name. We need to affirm with equal passion both the gloriously objective truth of verse 17, and the searching personal truth of verse 18.

THE CONFUSED NEBUCHADNEZZAR

Then Nebuchadnezzar was furious with Shadrach, Meshach and Abednego, and his attitude towards them changed. He ordered the furnace to be heated seven times hotter than usual and commanded some of the strongest soldiers in his army to tie up Shadrach, Meshach and Abednego and throw them into the blazing furnace. So these men, wearing their robes, trousers, turbans and other clothes, were bound and thrown into the blazing furnace. The king's command was so urgent and the furnace so hot that the flames of the fire killed the soldiers who took up Shadrach, Meshach and Abednego, and these three men, firmly tied, fell into the blazing furnace.

Then King Nebuchadnezzar leaped to his feet in amazement and asked his advisers, 'Weren't there three men that we tied up and threw into the fire?'

They replied, 'Certainly, O king.'

He said, 'Look! I see four men walking around in the fire, unbound and unharmed, and the fourth looks like a son of the gods.'

Nebuchadnezzar then approached the opening of the blazing furnace and shouted, 'Shadrach, Meshach and Abednego, servants of the Most High God, come out! Come here!'

So Shadrach, Meshach and Abednego came out of the fire, and the satraps, prefects, governors and royal advisers crowded around them. They saw that the fire had not harmed their bodies, nor was a hair of their heads singed; their robes were not scorched, and there was no smell of fire on them.

Then Nebuchadnezzar said, 'Praise be to the God of Shadrach, Meshach and Abednego, who has sent his angel and rescued his servants! They trusted in him and defied the king's command and were willing to give up their lives rather than serve or worship any god except their own God. Therefore I decree that the people of any nation or language who say anything against the God of Shadrach, Meshach and Abednego be cut into pieces and their houses be turned into piles of rubble, for no other god can save in this way.'

Then the king promoted Shadrach, Meshach and Abednego in the province of Babylon.

Daniel 3:19–30

The fourth man in the flames! It is somewhat pointless to argue about his identity. It may seem easy for us, from our perspective, to say it must have been Christ.

The important thing in the story is, that from Nebuchadnezzar's point of view, it was 'one like a son of the gods' that is, a divine person, someone or something beyond all human comprehension or power, somebody from outside his experience or his control.

For Nebuchadnezzar, then, it was a shattering confrontation with the 'rock' of his worst nightmare. Who was this? What was this external power beyond all his puny efforts and threats? It was God of course, engaging in yet another episode of dealing with this man – a process which will come to a climax in the next chapter. It was obviously a highly emotional experience. Nebuchadnezzar is filled first with fury, then with fear, and finally falls into flattery. The closing verses of the chapter are hardly yet a conversion. More like a confusion! But for him it was certainly a disturbing encounter with the kingdom of God – a kingdom that so dramatically set limits to the power of his own.

And for the three friends, and all those of their spiritual lineage who read the story, it was simply proof of the truth of Isaiah 43:2, 'When you walk through the fire, you will not be burned'. You're never alone in the flames, whether you walk out alive or not. This is a truth that has brought comfort and courage to all persecuted believers, especially those who have had to live in the reality of verse 18 while affirming their faith in the God of verse 17.

4

HEAVEN RULES

. . . ON EARTH

I heard the other day that in a poll to discover the most hated figures in America (the things people have polls for!), among the top ten came . . . tele-evangelists. At one level, I find that healthy and encouraging. It shows that people are not entirely taken in by the prostitution of the gospel and the gross self-exaltation of human media manipulators. There are few manifestations of modern western Christianity that I find more distasteful or further removed from the teachings, example and life-style of Jesus of Nazareth. On the other hand, of course, there is a deep sadness that the name of Christ should be so smeared with the unpopularity of these false prophets and millionaire pedlars. That conflict of reactions to them gets even more muddled when, as has happened several times in recent years, some of them fall off their pedestals and are caught with more than their metaphorical pants down. It is hard not to see the hand of the God who is able to humble 'those who walk in pride' (Daniel 4:37). But it is also hard not to feel a twinge of relief, or something not far from gloating, when such mega figures are reduced to size and exposed as ordinary sinners like the rest of us. Then the sobering thought comes to those of us who know our own hearts at all that 'there, but for the grace of God, go I'. Gloating, like pride itself, tends to go before a fall.

For Christians in public life, coping with pride, in oneself or in others, can be difficult. Suppose we have to work within an authority structure which is oppressive and unpopular. How do we feel if an arrogant boss is sacked or demoted? Or suppose we find ourselves going from success to success. How then do we sort out godly ambitions from mere lust for power and position, or material advancement? Chapter four of Daniel is a colourful and very penetrating study of pride and humility, from various angles. And it is in a form that we instinctively tune in to – a testimony! Here we have Nebuchadnezzar's written testimony to whoever has ears to hear. He would have gone down well at a John Wimber rally!

> King Nebuchadnezzar,
>   To the peoples, nations and men of every
> language, who live in all the world:
>   May you prosper greatly!
>   It is my pleasure to tell you about the
> miraculous signs and wonders that the Most High
> God has performed for me.   *Daniel 4:1,2*

Like a good preacher, Nebuchadnezzar states the main point of his testimony at the beginning (v 3), summarizes it again at the end (v 34),and repeats it three times in the middle (vs 17, 25, 32). It is simply this, that the Most High God is king, and not just king in heaven: he rules among the kingdoms of men on earth. In short, 'heaven rules' (v 26). This is the lesson that Nebuchadnezzar finally learns by the end of this drama. The chapter is like a play with three main actors.

NEBUCHADNEZZAR THE BUILDER

> I, Nebuchadnezzar, was at home in my palace, contented and prosperous . . .
>
> Twelve months later, as the king was walking on the roof of the royal palace of Babylon, he said, 'Is not this the great Babylon I have built as the royal residence, by my mighty power and for the glory of my majesty?'   *Daniel 4:4, 29, 30*

Nebuchadnezzar was a builder in many different ways.

• *He built an empire*. Out of the tatters of Assyria and in competition with Egypt he built an empire that lasted some seventy years.
• *He built a culture*, known as the Neo-Babylonian culture to historians. It is perhaps reflected in the great music festival of Daniel 3.
• *He built an educated, multi-racial civil service*, as we saw in Daniel 1.
• *He built a city – Babylon*. He glorified and beautified it, so that it was not for nothing that the famous 'Hanging Gardens of Babylon' were among the Seven Wonders of the ancient world.

Altogether, it was a remarkable and creditable achievement. Humanly speaking, he had plenty to be pleased about and proud of – his boasting had its basis in fact, at least. Even theologically speaking, we need to recall that it was God who had raised him up and given him authority, power and wide dominion with all the wealth and opportunities that go along with such a position (cf Daniel 2:37, 38; 5:18). And he had used it all well, to great advantage. We know from Daniel 3 that there was a nasty side to Nebuchadnezzar, that he was not averse to cremating dissidents, but we need not exaggerate that out of proportion. By the standards of his own age, he was a competent, efficient and constructive ruler.

However, as so often, the Bible sees beyond and behind the external splendour to the reality as God knows it. It sees inside Nebuchadnezzar's heart to the pride that filled it, and underneath the glory of his city to the social evil that it was built on.

Nebuchadnezzar's was not just your ordinary, everyday kind of pride. He still had the budding delusions of divinity that we saw earlier in chapter three. He was still refusing to acknowledge what God had been trying to teach him for years, ever since Jeremiah had declared it publicly in that diplomatic conference (which Nebuchadnezzar must have known all about; his intelligence service was very good), where Jeremiah made it plain that all Nebuchadnezzar's power and authority were strictly *ex officio* as the 'servant of Yahweh' (Jeremiah 27:5–7).

Instead, Nebuchadnezzar was turning the gift of God to his own glory. Already we have seen in him a model of typical state arrogance and idolatrous totalitarianism – the classic human pride of great civilizations and collective human 'grand designs'. Here in Daniel 4 we see a model of human pride at the personal level.

There is something of a Nebuchadnezzar in most of us. Many people, of course, suffer from a low self-image (not Nebuchadnezzar's biggest problem!). Lack of self-worth can be a terribly crippling thing. But it is probably still true to say that pride is the commoner, and deadlier, sin. It is even possible, according to some Christian psychologists, that preoccupation with low self-image may in itself conceal a form of pride, or at least ego-centredness. I remember a rather arrogant person once being described as a person who is fighting a low self-image – and winning!

David Myers and Malcolm Jeeves (in *Psychology through the Eyes of Faith*, Apollos, 1991) present the findings of various pieces of research that reveal the pervasiveness of the self-serving bias in human nature. They describe the 'self-centred filter' through which people explain their experiences. This has the effect of taking credit when we succeed, but attributing failure to external circumstances. They say that in published surveys of self-ratings, most of us believe we are better than average in every sphere researched. They comment on the difficulties we all have in accepting we have made a mistake, combined with energetic attempts to justify or defend ourselves.

> Human nature is governed by a totalitarian ego that continually revises the past in order to preserve a positive self-evaluation. Because of our mind's powers of reconstruction, we can be sure, argues Mike Yaconelli, that 'Every moving illustration,

every gripping story, every testimony, didn't happen (at least, it didn't happen like the storyteller said it happened).' Every anecdotal recollection told by a Christian superstar is a reconstruction. It's a point worth remembering in times when we are feeling disenchanted by the comparative ordinariness of our everyday lives. *(pp 131–132)*

Myers and Jeeves go on to point out the serious consequences of pride, in terms that this chapter of Daniel fully confirm.

The Bible does warn us against self-righteous pride – pride that alienates us from God and leads us to disdain one another. Such pride is at the heart of racism, sexism, nationalism, and all the deadly chauvinisms that lead one group of people to see themselves as more moral, deserving, or able than another. The flip side of being proud of our individual and group achievements, and taking credit for them, is blaming the poor for their poverty and the oppressed for their oppression.

(p 135)

We are all building something. It may be our own personal little empire, or just our own little nest. It may be our career, our project, or our business. It may even be our 'ministry', if we are in so-called 'full-time Christian work'. There is no sign saying 'Nebuchadnezzars keep out' over the door of the work we believe (or claim) we are doing for God. And the more God gives to us, the greater our natural and spiritual gifts, the more resources he puts at our disposal to build with, the greater is the temptation to play Nebuchadnezzars. In fact, the more gifted you are, the more dangerous you are. It is tragic that the world of Christian ministry and mission is littered with bloated egos and wonderful gifts being prostituted to the idols of pride.

'Is not this a great institution that I have built up?'

'Is not this a great movement that I have launched?'

'Is this not a great mission that I have helped to found.'

'Is this not a great business that (with God's help, of course) I have helped to prosper?'

It disturbs me greatly that so many Christian foundations, funds, colleges and schools, ministries and missions, are built on a person's own name (usually with 'International', or 'Incorporated' spliced on the end for even more effect). It distressed Martin Luther very much that people were calling churches by his name. He never wanted there to be a 'Lutheran' church, when Christ was its only Lord. Even the Apostle Paul rebuked the Corinthians for the misuse of human names as labels for factionalism and pride.

And yet, of course, I have to be scrupulously honest here. I have to admit myself that, while I certainly pray that the books I write will be a blessing, a means of grace and growth, and bring glory to Christ, I am certainly pleased that my name is on the front of them. When I speak at Christian jaunts and jamborees, of course I want to preach and teach for God's glory, but it would be dishonest to deny that I enjoy seeing my name on the programmes. Not one of us is immune to the temptations of pride, to scheming and building for our own advantage, success or reputation. Only as this universal tendency is honestly recognized, confessed and kept open before God can we hope to walk in humility with God and others. Otherwise, like Nebuchadnezzar, we may find that God may have to intervene in less pleasant ways to humble us and bring us back to sanity. So, in the next act of this drama, we find that God, in his final move to bring Nebuchadnezzar to his senses, resorts to two familiar tools: a well-tested method, dreams; and a well-trusted messenger, Daniel. As in Daniel 2, Nebuchadnezzar is disturbed by a weird and threatening nightmare, which shattered his complacent ease. Notice the sudden change.

> I, Nebuchadnezzar, was at home in my palace, contented and prosperous. I had a dream that made me afraid. As I was lying in my bed, the images and visions that passed through my mind terrified me. So I commanded that all the wise men of Babylon be brought before me to interpret the dream for me. When the magicians, enchanters, astrologers and diviners came, I told them the dream, but they could not interpret it for me. Finally, Daniel came into my presence and I told him the dream. (He is called Belteshazzar, after the name of my god, and the spirit of the holy gods is in him.) *Daniel 4:4–8*

All the wise men of Babylon troop on stage to do their stuff but, not unexpectedly, prove as incompetent as ever and so make their exit even more promptly, and Daniel enters to hushed whispers of expectancy from the audience.

DANIEL, THE CHALLENGER

Nebuchadnezzar loses no time in telling Daniel his dream.

'Belteshazzar, chief of the magicians, I know that the spirit of the holy gods is in you, and no mystery is too difficult for you. Here is my dream; interpret it for me. These are the visions I saw while lying in my bed: I looked, and there before me stood a tree in the middle of the land. Its height was enormous. The tree grew large and strong and its top touched the sky; it was visible to the ends of the earth. Its leaves were beautiful, its fruit abundant, and on it was food for all. Under it the beasts of the field found shelter, and the birds of the air lived in its branches; from it every creature was fed.

'In the visions I saw while lying in my bed, I looked, and there before me was a messenger, a holy one, coming down from heaven. He called in a loud voice: "Cut down the tree and trim off its branches; strip off its leaves and scatter its fruit. Let the animals flee from under it and the birds from its branches. But let the stump and its roots, bound with iron and bronze, remain in the ground, in the grass of the field.

' "Let him be drenched with the dew of heaven, and let him live with the animals among the plants of the earth. Let his mind be changed from that of a man and let him be given the mind of an animal, till seven times pass by for him.

' "The decision is announced by messengers, the holy ones declare the verdict, so that the living may know that the Most High is sovereign over the kingdoms of men and gives them to anyone he wishes and sets over them the lowliest of men."

'This is the dream that I, King Nebuchadnezzar,

had. Now, Belteshazzar, tell me what it means, for none of the wise men in my kingdom can interpret it for me. But you can, because the spirit of the holy gods is in you.'

Daniel 4:9–18

There are two features of Daniel's response to the king's dream.

His pastoral concern

It seems that the bond established between Daniel and Nebuchadnezzar as a result of his last bout of insomnia in Daniel 2 had lasted throughout his reign. Once again, we should marvel at the fact that Daniel so freely, so willingly, so competently served the man who had destroyed his homeland, devastated his city and deported his people. We could hardly have a more practical example of 'Love your enemies' in Old Testament dress. Daniel was only resident in Babylon by force. He had not asked to be sent there. He was, at best, a conscript missionary. He could have settle down to a life of permanent bitterness and a disgruntled attitude towards both God and his Babylonian lords, masters and neighbours. But he did not, and the fact that he did not meant that he was now able to speak a word from God to his troubled, pagan king.

Elaine was a physiotherapist in a British hospital. She enjoyed her work and the department she was in. Then she got sent to a geriatric unit where she knew that those in charge were particularly coarse in their manner and conversation. She was most reluctant to go, but had little choice. Sure enough, daily life became difficult and embarrassing. Things were said and done in a way that she knew were deliberately meant to upset or provoke her as a Christian. But she prayed for the grace to keep cool, to respond as she hoped Christ would have. In the end, to her relief, she was transferred, feeling something of a failure as a witness. However, she later discovered that both the people concerned had been silently impressed with her attitude and response to their behaviour, and one of them has since joined a group exploring the Christian faith. God had a purpose in putting her through the agony of such a placement, but it could only be fulfilled through her willingness to live with it. It could transform our attitude to the world of work if we looked on every move or transfer – wanted or unwanted, welcome or unwelcome – as an implicit missionary task, however inadequate we may feel for it.

I also think Daniel's life was an example of Jesus' command to 'pray for those who persecute you'. I imagine that Daniel, since he was among the first batch of exiles, would have read the letter Jeremiah sent to the exiles in Babylon, way back before the final destruction of Jerusalem, telling them to *pray for Babylon!*

> This is what the LORD Almighty, the God of Israel, says to all those I carried into exile from Jerusalem to Babylon: '. . . seek the peace and prosperity of the city to which I have carried you into exile. Pray to the LORD for it, because if it prospers, you too will prosper.'
> *Jeremiah 29:4,7*

We know that Daniel was a man of prayer, with the

habit of praying three times daily (Daniel 6:10). I wonder if Nebuchadnezzar was top of his prayer list? For Daniel, serving the king was actually a means of serving the God who had appointed the king, and that was a perspective forged and preserved by regular prayer. Prayer sets our thinking straight and fosters the kind of maturity which we see in Daniel here – a maturity which had grown beyond a desire for revenge, or a simple racial or religious hatred, and which could perceive the voice of God once again in the mind of his pagan political boss.

Think of the situation from Daniel's point of view. There you are, standing listening to a dream in which a huge tree gets chopped down, somebody gets driven out to eat grass with the cattle, a voice pronounces divine judgement upon him . . . and suddenly you realise that it all applies to the man who is telling you his dream – the king himself.

Nebuchadnezzar is for the chop! Wouldn't you have inwardly cheered? Wouldn't you have gloated, 'And about time too!'? Wouldn't you have silently praised God for letting you live long enough to see his long-awaited revenge on this beast of a man who had raped and pillaged his holy city and bulldozed and burnt his temple? Such reactions would be perfectly understandable. But they were not Daniel's.

> Then Daniel (also called Belteshazzar) was greatly perplexed for a time, and his thoughts terrified him. So the king said, 'Belteshazzar, do not let the dream or its meaning alarm you.'
> Belteshazzar answered, 'My lord, if only the dream applied to your enemies and its meaning to your adversaries!' *Daniel 4:19*

He was dismayed. He could not bear to tell the king. He could only wish what the king was probably secretly hoping – that the dream applied to his enemies, though Daniel knew it did not. It was for Nebuchadnezzar, and must be faithfully interpreted. But he did so reluctantly, pastorally. Daniel had gone beyond malice and vengeance, and could take no pleasure in the destruction of the wicked. Again, this seems to me to be the mark of a person who has become like the God he spends time in prayer with.

If it is a test of our maturity how we deal with pride in ourselves, it is equally so when we have to handle pride – or its downfall – in others. The instinct for revenge is very strong. We long to see the arrogant and prosperous brought down a peg or three. But how do we react when they are? Then the true motives of our hearts are exposed. Then it will be seen whether we reflect a self-righteous rejoicing in another human being's frailty, or a Christ-like sorrow over those who even betray and deny him.

His prophetic courage

It took courage for Daniel to interpret the dream faithfully, to say to the most powerful man on earth, 'You are that tree . . .' (v 22); to tell this monarch of all he surveyed that he would soon be sharing food with the beasts of the field; to tell this 'head of gold', always accustomed to looking down from the top of his statue to the lesser mortals below, that he must look up and acknowledge a higher king than himself; to direct his attention to the reign of the Most High God before it was too late. Another New Testament command about 'speaking the truth in love' (Ephesians 4:15) finds its Old Testament model here also.

But even more courage was needed for what Daniel said next. He goes beyond straight interpretation of the dream and the words that were part of it, and risks a word of his own.

'Therefore, O king, be pleased to accept my advice . . .' (v 27). Now Nebuchadnezzar hadn't asked for any advice. The simple interpretation of the dream was unwelcome enough. But Daniel risks it. It shows, I think, that he had confidence in the king's respect for him, which matched his own pastoral concern and personal respect for the king. And the word he spoke took all the authentic strength of a prophet to deliver, which was not familiar ground for Daniel. He was no professional prophet. He was a civil servant, and civil servants are not notorious for hazarding risky opinions to their overlords.

Daniel put his finger on the sore spot of Babylon's imperial glory – its social costs in terms of oppression and exploitation. He could see at first hand what the prophet Habakkuk had condemned when, speaking about Babylon, he had delivered words of divine rebuke and judgement:

> 'Woe to him who piles up stolen goods
>   and makes himself wealthy by extortion!
>   How long must this go on?'

> 'Woe to him who builds his realm by unjust gain
>   to set his nest on high,
>   to escape the clutches of ruin!'

> 'Woe to him who builds a city with bloodshed
>   and establishes a town by crime!'
>
> *Habakkuk 2:6, 9, 12*

So Daniel had the courage to call Nebuchadnezzar both to personal repentance and to social reform, in ringing, razor sharp words that an Amos would have been proud of:

> 'Therefore, O king, be pleased to accept my advice: Renounce your sins by doing what is right, and your wickedness by being kind to the oppressed. It may be that then your prosperity will continue.'
>
> *Daniel 4:27*

This makes it very clear that Nebuchadnezzar's sin, in the eyes of God, was not merely personal pride and arrogant delusions of grandeur, but actual, practical injustice and oppression in the social realm. So the word of God to him had to be more than just, 'Confess your sins and get your attitude right'. He had to change, and to prove this change of heart by a change in official state policy, to replace exploitation with justice and kindness.

There is a sharp irony in the words Nebuchadnezzar says in verse 30. 'Is not this the great Babylon which *I* have built . . . ?' *He had built?* Nebuchadnezzar probably never handled a brick in his life. *He* had not built Babylon. It had been built by the sweat of the nameless thousands of oppressed slaves, immigrants and other poor sections of the nation, whose labours have built every vaunting civilization of the fallen human race in history. The God of Daniel saw, heard, and was concerned, just as he had heard the outcry coming up from Sodom and Gomorrah (Genesis 18:20, 21, cf Ezekiel 16:49), just as he had heard the groaning of his own people in Egypt (Exodus 2:23, 24). Daniel also, his ear attuned to the mind of his God, felt the heartbeat of the God whose commitment to the poor and oppressed was part of his spiritual heritage, history and worship.

> [The LORD] upholds the cause of the oppressed
>   and gives food to the hungry.
> The LORD sets prisoners free,
>   the LORD gives sight to the blind,
> The LORD lifts up those who are bowed down,
>   the LORD loves the righteous.
> The LORD watches over the alien
>   and sustains the fatherless and the widow,
>   but he frustrates the ways of the wicked.
>
> The LORD reigns for ever,
>   your God, O Zion, for all generations.
> Praise the LORD.   *Psalm 146:7–10*

We should not miss the tremendous drama of this moment in Daniel's life. Here was a civil servant – albeit a respected one, with the probably not very welcome title, 'Chief of the Magicians' (v 9) – standing before the supreme head of state, challenging him in the name of God on the whole social and economic direction of his state policy. People have lost their heads for far less than that – John the Baptist lost his for criticising a petty king over his marriage! And Daniel not only challenges, he calls the head of state to repent, with the explicit threat that if he does not, he will face humiliation. His words may have been padded out a bit with the official civil service politeness – 'Be pleased to accept my advice', and all that – but they packed a lethal punch. Daniel faced the king with the social wickedness of his government and called on him to grasp the nettle of reform – or eat the nettles of his punishment.

By the end of this story, one of the things which Nebuchadnezzar finally admits about the God he has encountered is his justice: 'everything [God] does is right and all his ways are just' (Daniel 4:37), which may be a way of saying that Nebuchadnezzar now knows what *he* must do to follow up his submission to God. *But who put that idea in his head in the first place?* Daniel – years before. Daniel, who not only had the courage to speak the truth to the king, but *who was also in a position to speak it.* In other words, Daniel was only able to speak this word of challenge and rebuke, which ultimately led to the king's conversion, because he had spent a lifetime of faithful service in the secular administration of this alien country. How does that sound to us who are used to instant results? A lifetime's secular job – a moment's opportunity to speak the challenging prophetic word to the key person at the right time.

When you think back to Daniel 1, and the decisions that Daniel and his three friends took in their youth, you can see how much depended on these decisions later. Their decision to say 'No' on the (probable) issue of total allegiance to the state led them into the fiery furnace, only to prove there the power of their God. But their decision to say 'Yes' to the programme of training and the administrative career meant that Daniel was in the right place at the right time when the prophetic word needed to be spoken right into the ear of the political power. If Daniel had not said 'Yes' at the beginning of his career, he would not have been in a position to speak at all. If he had not said 'No', he would not have had the critical distance to deliver the kind of challenging word that he did. If he and his friends had opted out of public secular life altogether, they could have had no impact or witness in relation to it. If they had been co-opted in as mere stooges of the government, they would have had no prophetic leverage to say anything that cut across official policy. They were in the world, but they had not sold their souls to the world.

I believe there is a word of tremendous encouragement here to Christians who work in the secular world. As someone who has lived the coward's life of a Christian environment, first in ordained pastoral ministry in the Church of England, then as a missionary in India but living and working in a Christian college there, and now in a community of people training for cross-cultural mission, I have a very profound respect for Christians who stick it out in all kinds of secular jobs, and especially those who are in public or political service of any kind. You are the real 'salt of the earth' in the sense that Jesus meant. You are those who stand against corruption and shine as lights in the midst of 'a crooked and depraved generation' (Philippians 2:15). You are Daniels *in situ*.

Yet so often the church gives the impression that what really counts is 'the ministry' or 'missionary work', when in fact it is the presence and faithful work and witness of the hosts of Christian so-called 'lay people' that matters far, far more in relation to the world around us. This is why I generally prefer speaking at conferences of Christians in secular professions and jobs, than at clergy or theological student gatherings. There is a sense of reality. There is an awareness of the sharp and rough edges of life. There is a wrestling with agonizing dilemmas. There is also a healthy refusal to let the tame theologian present get away with any vague answers that don't engage with the real issues.

And my word to such groups is always to get them to grasp that ministry and mission in God's world are far too important to be left to ministers and missionaries. Daniel had a mission but it took him a lifetime of hard work in a government office to fulfil it. He earned the respect of the king and the right to speak, and when the moment came, he had the courage to speak it in the name of God. So wherever God has put you and whatever your daily grind, see it as the place where you may be called to be the spark-plug where the power of God's word jumps explosively across the gap into the secular world.

GOD, THE HUMBLER

God gave Nebuchadnezzar twelve months – a whole year to act on the implications of his dream and its courageous interpretation by Daniel; a year to do something in response to the advice and the warning he had been given. But he ignored it all. In verses 29 and 30 we find him quite unchanged.

> Twelve months later, as the king was walking on the roof of the royal palace of Babylon, he said, 'Is not this the great Babylon I have built as the royal residence, by my mighty power and for the glory of my majesty?'
> *Daniel 4:29, 30*

At last God moves in to his final act to humble this man and bring him to his senses. Nebuchadnezzar had delusions of being more than human, so, with a kind of poetic justice, God sent him delusions of being less than human! The delusion of thinking oneself to be a particular animal and behaving as such is a known form of mental illness.

> The words were still on his lips when a voice came from heaven, 'This is what is decreed for you, King Nebuchadnezzar: Your royal authority has been taken from you. You will be driven away from people and will live with the wild animals; you will eat grass like cattle. Seven times will pass by for you until you acknowledge that the Most High is sovereign over the kingdoms of men and gives them to anyone he wishes.'
>
> Immediately what had been said about Nebuchadnezzar was fulfilled. He was driven away from people and ate grass like cattle. His body was drenched with the dew of heaven until his hair grew like the feathers of an eagle and his nails like the claws of a bird. *Daniel 4:31–33*

The fact of the twelve month delay in carrying out the threat of the dream shows God's own reluctance. God took no pleasure in reducing a human being, made in his own image, to the level of a brute beast. God wants humility, not humiliation. But, if necessary, he will humiliate the proud into genuine humility if there is no other way. Not only is he able to humble 'those who walk in pride' (v 37), but it is characteristic of him to do so (cf Proverbs 3:34 and its application in James 4:1–10).

The humiliation lasted only as long as it took Nebuchadnezzar to learn his lesson. 'Seven times' is a deliberately vague phrase – it need not mean seven years. So
what was it he needed to learn? The three-times-
repeated truth, which forms the theme of this whole
chapter that the Most High God rules over the kingdoms of men. Nebuchadnezzar, head of a human kingdom, was up against the kingdom of God and it was
an uncomfortable experience to say the least.

Nebuchadnezzar would certainly have accepted
that the Most High God ruled in heaven. No problem
about that; that's what a god is for. Let him rule in
heaven all he likes – so long as he stays there. But the
point he could not take was that the God of heaven
rules *on earth*. The reign of God is 'earthed' among the
kingdoms of men. This point was bowled at him in his
first dream in the shape of the rock which toppled all
human empires and grew to fill the whole earth. Daniel
told him then that this portrayed the rule of God which
was indestructible. But Nebuchadnezzar had not fielded
it. He would not accept that heaven rules – on earth.
So he had felt free to build his city and empire on
injustice and oppression. When human beings act without any sense of a higher authority, with no sense of
accountability to God, then both individually and as a
society we are capable of terrible cruelty to one another.
Individual pride and state pride get out of control when
they are unchecked by any submission to a transcendent
authority.

This is one reason why the *real* Jesus was and is
so uncomfortable to many. Jesus challenged the people
of his day to recognize that the reign of God was among
them. In his teaching and parables he showed that it

was a kingdom that turned the world's values upside down. It cut across the political drift of his nation. It cut across the economic values that led to wealth for some, and debt and poverty for others. It cut across personal attitudes and behaviour that excluded and marginalized whole categories of people. The only way to cope with such a kingdom was to submit, repent, accept it and live a radically changed life – or to resist it and be destroyed.

It is also why when the church of today tries to make people acknowledge the presence of the kingdom of God, by holding them morally accountable for public policies and their social consequences, it becomes unpopular. No government cheerfully accepts criticism, least of all from 'interfering clergy'. Let the clergy stay in their pulpits and stick to spiritual matters. Let God stay in heaven and keep it warm till we all get there. This is how the state and its political servants would prefer things to stay. That way, we can get on with preserving the unjust *status quo*, unchecked by uncomfortable notions of a living God who might call us to account.

Finally, however, Nebuchadnezzar saw the truth that God had been trying to teach him for years.

> At the end of that time, I, Nebuchadnezzar, raised my eyes towards heaven, and my sanity was restored. Then I praised the Most High; I honoured and glorified him who lives for ever.
> His dominion is an eternal dominion;
> his kingdom endures from generation to
> generation. *Daniel 4:34*

It is interesting how an attack of humility also led to sanity! Pride, especially the kind of pride that tries to get away with ignoring God and his demands, is really a kind of madness. To live in God's world and behave as if we have the right to own it, and treat others as we like without reference to him, is mad! Even to try to live our everyday life and work as if God was only for Sundays is asking for trouble. God refuses to be sidelined like that, and we need to walk in humility before him, willing to say, as Nebuchadnezzar now virtually said, 'Your kingdom come, your will be done, *on earth as in heaven.*' For it is still true that 'those who walk in pride [God] is able to humble' (v 37). But he would infinitely rather that we humble ourselves first.

5

BLASPHEMY –
ANCIENT
AND MODERN

If you are a businessman and you've been failing to meet your targets, you may find yourself 'weighed in the balance and found wanting'. If the situation gets worse, you could be told that 'your days are numbered'. It could even be that 'the writing is on the wall' for your company. All three proverbs of failure and impending doom are derived from Daniel 5. It is a very dark chapter indeed – all the more so coming after chapter four, with its ringing testimony and happy ending.

THE BLASPHEMY OF BELSHAZZAR

King Belshazzar gave a great banquet for a thousand of his nobles and drank wine with them. While Belshazzar was drinking his wine, he gave orders to

bring in the gold and silver goblets that
Nebuchadnezzar his father had taken from the
temple in Jerusalem, so that the king and his nobles,
his wives and his concubines might drink from them.
So they brought in the gold goblets that had been
taken from the temple of God in Jerusalem, and the
king and his nobles, his wives and his concubines
drank from them. As they drank the wine, they
praised the gods of gold and silver, of bronze, iron,
wood and stone. *Daniel 5:1–4*

There is no doubt that the author of the book wants us
to see a deliberately pointed contrast between Nebuchadnezzar and Belshazzar.

• Nebuchadnezzar was a builder (as we saw in the last
chapter). Belshazzar was a 'waster'. Here we find him
drunk and incapacitated at the very time when his
whole kingdom was under threat. Historically, Belshazzar was only the deputy ruler on behalf of Nabonidus,
who was the successor to Nebuchadnezzar. Nabonidus
was absent from Babylon at this moment, but the fact
that he was the real king explains why Belshazzar could
only offer the job of 'third highest ruler in the kingdom'
as a prize to the successful handwriting-on-wall expert
(Daniel 5:7). Belshazzar himself occupied the second
highest seat, but it is clear that the Babylonian empire
was being mismanaged and in terminal collapse.

• Nebuchadnezzar had some religious respect for the
holy things of other nations. He had taken the captured
vessels of the temple in Jerusalem and at least put them
in another temple – a sacred place for sacred objects

(Daniel 1:2). Belshazzar treated these same objects with intentional mockery and profanity.

What makes his action so offensive? These temple vessels were highly symbolic and emotive objects. Like the temple itself, they were associated with the presence and the holiness of the God of Israel. The temple was the earthly dwelling-place of God's name, and thus of his person, in the midst of his people. So the capture of the precious objects inside it symbolized not only the humiliation and defeat of Israel, but also must have been seen as proof of the inferiority of their God. Yahweh was a beaten and captured deity, and his sacred bits and pieces were stashed away in a pagan shrine. The sense of outrage and shame must have been as great as or greater than the appalling capture of the ark of the covenant by the Philistines many centuries earlier in the time of Eli (1 Samuel 4).

The temple vessels are mentioned with greater detail in several other places as well as at the beginning of the book of Daniel (2 Kings 25:13–15, 2 Chronicles 36:18). But it is clear that although their capture was a great national shame, the very fact that they were still *there*, somewhere, was a symbol of hope. In the early days of the exile there was an argument over them between Hananiah, a false prophet, who predicted that they would soon be back in Jerusalem, and Jeremiah, who replied that although he would like to believe that too, it simply wouldn't happen, not for a long, long time (Jeremiah 28). Jeremiah was right; and Hananiah, who said the vessels would be back within two years, was dead in two months.

So we need to understand that Belshazzar's blasphemy was not just that he showed some minor disrespect for a few sacred objects of another people's religion, like the thoughtlessness of a tourist who forgets to remove his shoes in the holy place of some foreign religion. It was rather a calculated and intentional mockery of what those vessels represented – the God of the Jews; the God of that wretched ethnic minority who were still derisively labelled 'the exiles of Judah' (Daniel 5:13, 6:13); the God who, in Belshazzar's eyes, was defeated more than a generation ago, and who was certainly powerless to do anything about a spot of teasing and taunting by his revelling young party set.

His blasphemy went further still. The text suggests that he had to be drunk to go this far. For it was not merely that he used the sacred vessels for ordinary drinking at his party. That would be distasteful in itself, rather like taking the church's communion silver and using it at a cheese and wine party. He did more than that. He and his cheering chums used these sacred goblets – goblets that had been used in the service of the only living God – to pour out drink offerings to other gods, lifeless gods, mere objects (Daniel 5:4)! In shock value, this was like using a church's communion table and vessels for occult, satanist rituals. The blatant sacrilege and idolatry in such action would draw gasps of disbelief from any Jewish listeners to the story. How could God tolerate such offence to his holiness? Well, he didn't for long, since the next word is 'Suddenly . . .'

But before we move on to God's intervention, we should pause and think a bit more about what we really mean by blasphemy in our day. Is it still a real thing? Does it happen? Does it matter?

Belshazzar's blasphemy consisted in taking what

belonged to the true and living God, and using it for his own corrupt and decadent purposes in a context of contempt for God's assumed powerlessness. He could use the name of Yahweh and the things of Yahweh for fun, pleasure or spite, believing that Yahweh was outdated, irrelevant and impotent. I think, when you look at it like that, blasphemy in the form of attitudes and actions like that is by no means dead in our world.

In British law, of course, blasphemy has only the specific significance of something which mocks or insults the Christian religion itself. There are those who argue that such a one-sided law should either be extended to include the religious sensibilities of all faiths in the land, including Muslims, Jews, Hindus etc, or else be abolished altogether. I must say that I tend to agree with this view. I do not think *Christ himself* needs the 'protection' of our human laws. But on the other hand it is perfectly right that the law should protect all citizens, of whatever faith, from unreasonable and gratuitous offence and distress.

However, there are more serious forms of blasphemy in our society which, like idolatry, are often unrecognized because we take them almost for granted.

The media

I think it is blasphemous, though I would put it at the less serious end of my scale, that the name of Christ, the cross itself, and other precious factors of the biblical faith, are so easily used in the media as expletives or as a source of comedy. The other night I watched a very talented British comedian, whom I normally enjoy immensely, using communion wine and wafer as props for a skit that combined the priesthood and sexual innuendo. I am not, I think, squeamish in my sense of humour. Certainly I do not think that we should never laugh at religion or sex. But I found the act uncomfortably close to blasphemy. The almost mindless use of divine names and Christian symbols in the media may not be deliberate mockery of what they stand for, but it is certainly based on the assumption that there is no reality behind words like 'God', 'Jesus', 'Christ', 'hell' etc, certainly nothing that matters. So perhaps the fact that such constant media misuse reflects and amplifies the cheapening and irrelevance of the Christian message in society in general makes it a more serious matter than my personal 'blasphemy scale' suggests.

Militarism

Although I love my country and believe that the human kaleidoscope of nations and ethnic diversity is a creation gift of God for us to enjoy, there is a kind of patriotism which is undeniably blasphemous, as we already observed in chapter three. I think it is more seriously blasphemous when the church uses the name of God and Christ to 'bless' weapons of war and destruction, or 'sanctifies' acts of war by claiming that 'God is on our side'. I am not at all comfortable with national or regimental flags inside or on top of churches.

Consumerism

I think it is blasphemous that Christmas and the name of Christ (nativity scenes, grottos, and all) have been hijacked by the gods of materialism. However, I see that as only one part of the wider blasphemy by which our society has sacrificed virtually all its principles on the altar of consumerism. We now live with a philosophy of 'the market' which is 'believed in' with quasi-religious commitment and under which we are 'customers' in every walk of life. Moral values such as compassion, and social values such as education, are all quantified in monetary terms and subjected to market competition. The sick are no longer patients; they are customers whom hospitals must compete to win. The young are no longer pupils and students; they are customers whom schools and universities must compete to attract. (Even passengers are always customers now, with more justification, though they never ride on trains any more, but on 'services'.)

When will charities start calling their projects and beneficiaries 'customers'? Will worshippers become customers of the church? Since the rest of life is so ego-centred, it is hardly surprising that people compare churches according to which will give them the best deal for their own private needs. So we have politics for your greeds and religion for your needs. In a world where Mammon is god, such blasphemy is not inconceivable, for the name of God himself can be enlisted to serve Mammon, as the charlatans of the church in every age have proved, from Tetzel selling his indulgences for buying forgiveness in the sixteenth century, to tele-evangelists selling salvation, healing and prosperity in the twentieth. There are certainly Christian organizations in all parts of the world which have used the sacred commission of God to his church, to preach and teach and heal and feed, as a means to amass money for the benefit of those who run them. And others who have prostituted that commission into one vast entertainment industry for the already converted.

Pluralism

Then there is perhaps the hardest reflection of all on Belshazzar's blasphemy – its mixing of the things of the living God with the names of idols. The world of Daniel 5 was a world of religious plurality, where polytheism was the accepted creed and monotheism the butt of mockery. It didn't matter which god you worshipped so long as you didn't claim he was the only one, as the ridiculous 'exiles of Judah' believed. Not a lot has changed. The story has a pungent relevance to the multi-faith issue in contemporary society.

But it is a relevance that has to be very carefully and sensitively expressed. Some people would view any concession to other religions as a compromise in loyalty to Christ, if not strictly blasphemous. They would oppose, for example, the sale of redundant church buildings to Sikhs or any other faith. They would condemn even private prayer with a Muslim as well as public acts of multi-faith worship.

I would want to be more discriminating. It is one thing, I think, to treat a certain place or building with reverence while it is being used by a living community of Christian believers for regular worship. It is another thing to regard it as somehow sacrosanct even if it is no longer fulfilling that function, just because it has gothic windows or a steeple of sorts. The church is people, not bricks or stones. So if 'the church' has moved on or declined to the point of expiry, it is sad, but nothing is served by nostalgically hanging on to museum-piece buildings.

Furthermore, there is a Christian duty to love our neighbours, and that means respecting their choices and what is precious to them, even when we radically disagree. We have to see the distinction between having a commitment to the uniqueness of Christ and the truth of God's revelation through him on the one hand, and adopting negative and hostile attitudes to *people* who hold other religious beliefs on the other hand. The cause of the gospel is not served by hostility and obstructiveness.

In September 1987, a group of Christians living in a poor quarter on the outskirts of Bangalore, India, discovered that a whole community of Muslims had been evicted from their slum in another part of the city and dumped down in their area, with almost no provision for their needs. Among the things the Christians did to help the new, disorientated arrivals, was to help them get land for a mosque and also to help them build it. Now that might seem a strange strategy for mission to comfortable, outside observers like us. But the result was goodwill and harmonious relationships between the communities, on which quiet but fruitful opportunities for evangelism could later be built.

What is much more serious in my view, is when a place of living Christian worship is used for multi-faith services. Then a place, facilities and persons who have been consecrated to the service of the living God, in the name of Jesus Christ, are being used in forms of worship which use other names for deity and do not approach him or them through Christ. Then we are going far beyond the biblical requirement of neighbourliness.

Then we are making an implicit statement that other names for God (or no names at all) are equally valid, and that God can be acceptably worshipped other than through Christ and by way of his cross. *That*, in my view, *is* blasphemy.

But the more serious blasphemy is committed not necessarily by the worshippers at such an event of multifaith worship, who are probably participating in great, though misguided, sincerity, but by those Christian theologians and church leaders who justify such events by a pluralist theory of religions. It is all right, they say, to mingle Christian worship with the worship of other religions, because in the end we are all one. So they are happy to take the goblets of the living God of the Bible and pour drink offerings with them to other deities, claiming that there is really no difference. As Belshazzar despised and rejected the uniqueness of Yahweh, so such people dispense with the uniqueness of Christ. For to name his name on a par with other names, human or divine, is to dishonour him.

The fate that overtook Belshazzar is not one we would wish on anyone, no matter what their blasphemy. But it is a solemn object lesson in the truth that 'God is not mocked', and that his judgment is certain – whether it leads to repentance as in the case of Nebuchadnezzar in Daniel 4, or simply destruction as here.

> Suddenly the fingers of a human hand appeared and wrote on the plaster of the wall, near the lampstand in the royal palace. The king watched the hand as it wrote. His face turned pale and he was so frightened that his knees knocked together and his legs gave way.

BLASPHEMY – ANCIENT AND MODERN

The king called out for the enchanters, astrologers and diviners to be brought and said to these wise men of Babylon, 'Whoever reads this writing and tells me what it means will be clothed in purple and have a gold chain placed around his neck, and he will be made the third highest ruler in the kingdom.'

Then all the king's wise men came in, but they could not read the writing or tell the king what it meant. So King Belshazzar became even more terrified and his face grew more pale. His nobles were baffled.   *Daniel 5:5–9*

THE PROPHECY OF DANIEL

At least Nebuchadnezzar was allowed to have his nightmares in the privacy of his bedroom. Belshazzar is confronted with the in-breaking word of God in public. The finger of God that scattered plagues on Pharaoh (Exodus 8:19), that carved the ten commandments (Exodus 31:18, Deuteronomy 9:10), that would later drive out demons (Luke 11:20), takes visible form and writes mysteriously on the wall. The king is transformed from sacrilegious revelry to shaking panic and collapse.

Once again we are treated to the comic spectacle of the parade of the magicians, and once again they don't disappoint us. They are as useless as ever. 'All the king's horses and all the king's men couldn't put the royal knees together again!' Incompetence, of course, has never been a disqualification for high political office.

The preliminary speeches introducing Daniel to the

action, by the queen and Belshazzar himself, are more fulsome than ever. If we did not know that the king was in a state of drunken terror, his words of praise would sound almost deliberately sarcastic. The real irony is that he is now begging for help from one of the very people whose God he had been insulting only moments before.

The queen, hearing the voices of the king and his nobles, came into the banquet hall. 'O king, live for ever!' she said. "Don't be alarmed! Don't look so pale! There is a man in your kingdom who has the spirit of the holy gods in him. In the time of your father he was found to have insight and intelligence and wisdom like that of the gods. King Nebuchadnezzar your father – your father the king, I say – appointed him chief of the magicians, enchanters, astrologers and diviners. This man Daniel, whom the king called Belteshazzar, was found to have a keen mind and knowledge and understanding, and also the ability to interpret dreams, explain riddles and solve difficult problems. Call for Daniel, and he will tell you what the writing means.'

So Daniel was brought before the king, and the king said to him, 'Are you Daniel, one of the exiles my father the king brought from Judah? I have heard that the spirit of the gods is in you and that you have insight, intelligence and outstanding wisdom. The wise men and enchanters were brought before me to read this writing and tell me what it means, but they could not explain it. Now I have heard that you are able to give interpretations and to solve difficult problems. If you can read this writing and tell me what it means, you will be clothed in purple

> and have a gold chain placed around your neck, and
> you will be made the third highest ruler in the
> kingdom.'
> *Daniel 5:10–16*

So Daniel arrives. By this time, following the sequence
and chronology of the stories so far, he must have been
a very elderly man, probably in his eighties. He had
been brought to Babylon before the fall of Jerusalem in
587 BC and he is now just about to witness the fall of
Babylon in 539 BC. Yet here he is, still in government
service, as he had been for over fifty years, still available
to a drunken crown prince, still as courageous as ever.
Brushing aside the offers of material and political
reward – which he no longer needed – he delivers a
searing word of divine judgment on the drunken, drivel-
ling royal before him, before he even deigns to read and
interpret the writing on the wall as requested.

There is a striking contrast between his stance here
and the way he handled Nebuchadnezzar's problem in
Daniel 4. There, as we saw, his approach had a pastoral
warmth – a reluctant but truthful interpretation of the
dream, followed by urgent advice to repent and change
in the hope of avoiding the falling blow of judgment.
Here, he delivers a more characteristically prophetic
message – a direct word of outraged divine justice and
holiness to a man who was deliberately mocking God,
climaxing in a final word of inescapable doom.

> 'O king, the Most High God gave your father
> Nebuchadnezzar sovereignty and greatness and
> glory and splendour. Because of the high position he
> gave him, all the peoples and nations and men of
> every language dreaded and feared him. Those the
> king wanted to put to death, he put to death; those
> he wanted to spare, he spared; those he wanted to

promote, he promoted; and those he wanted to humble, he humbled. But when his heart became arrogant and hardened with pride, he was deposed from his royal throne and stripped of his glory. He was driven away from people and given the mind of an animal; he lived with the wild donkeys and ate grass like cattle; and his body was drenched with the dew of heaven, until he acknowledged that the most High God is sovereign over the kingdoms of men and sets over them anyone he wishes.

'But you his son, O Belshazzar, have not humbled yourself, though you knew all this. Instead, you have set yourself up against the Lord of heaven. You had the goblets from his temple brought to you, and you and your nobles, your wives and your concubines drank wine from them. You praised the gods of silver and gold, of bronze, iron, wood and stone, which cannot see or hear or understand. But you did not honour the God who holds in his hand your life and all your ways. Therefore he sent the hand that wrote the inscription.'   *Daniel 5:18–24*

There are two aspects of Daniel's speech to Belshazzar.

The lesson he would not learn

Daniel recalls what had happened to Nebuchadnezzar. The events were still very clear in his mind, even though it had happened several years earlier. Nebuchadnezzar was not Belshazzar's actual father; there had been a couple of short reigns between his death and the reign of Nabonidus for whom Belshazzar was now deputising as crown prince. But 'your father Nebuchadnezzar' was a standard way of referring to the illustrious ancestor.

Daniel also repeats the theological truth on which his whole relationship to Nebuchadnezzar had been built. It was God himself who had raised up the Babylonian king and given him human sovereignty over the whole ancient Near East. His power and glory were God's gift. But because he refused to acknowledge the fact, they became his downfall. And so, as we saw in Daniel 4, it took a searing and humiliating mental illness to make Nebuchadnezzar acknowledge the real identity and sovereignty of God. All this Daniel spells out, probably to the great impatience of the drunken crowd, still goggle-eyed at the writing on the wall.

Then comes the fatal blow: '*Though you knew all this . . .*' (v 22). Belshazzar had fully known all the facts about his famous ancestor's glorious reign, and the ignominious period of madness. He would also have known, perhaps even read, Nebuchadnezzar's proclamation with its testimony to the living reality of the Most High God whose kingdom rules over all human kings (and princes). He would have known the ominous warning at the end of that testimony that 'those who walk in pride he is able to humble' (Daniel 4:37). He knew all this. He knew the truth. But it all made no difference. He still went ahead with his arrogant mockery of the living God who had so humbled his predecessor.

The sin of Belshazzar, in other words, was sin against the light, sin against the truth, sin against the grace of having had an example and a lesson that he knew clearly. And such deliberate, open-eyed sin is the most serious kind. In its extreme form, it becomes what Jesus called 'sin against the Holy Spirit'. This is when a person, having seen and known the power of God at work, refuses to acknowledge him and instead attributes it to Satan or evil. The kind of moral and spiritual inversion necessary to reach that state makes it impossible for the person to recognize evil, repent of it, and thus be forgiven. That is why Jesus said that such sin will not be forgiven.

The God he would not honour

Far from learning the lesson that Nebuchadnezzar had learnt (the hard way), Belshazzar 'set himself up against the Lord of heaven' (v 23). In the light of chapter four, the very idea of doing such a thing seems foolhardy. And Daniel can point to the evidence for his accusation. He was not talking just about inner pride or mental attitudes. The goblets that had been used to pour libations to lifeless gods, in mockery of the living God to whom they belonged, were still rolling and dripping on the tables. If Nebuchadnezzar had been judged for mere words that passed his lips, how much more did Belshazzar deserve for such deliberate and practical blasphemy?

Nebuchadnezzar had finally been prepared to admit that he owed everything to God, but Belshazzar would not even credit God with his next breath. 'You did not honour the God who holds in his hand your life and all your ways' (v 24). One pictures Belshazzar slumped in his chair, still clutching in his hand some figurine of an idol, unaware that he himself is held in the very hand of the God he has mocked. 'It is a dreadful thing,' said the author of Hebrews, speaking about deliberate sinning that is contemptuous of God's grace, 'to fall into the hands of the living God' (Hebrews 10:31).

Belshazzar is a model of what the human race in general tends to do. One of the original marks of our fallen-ness is our refusal to honour God. Knowing the truth about God, we choose to deny it. And the more we go on doing so, the more we come to believe our own lies, until we reach the point where the truth itself is regarded as falsehood, while our own lies are paraded as absolute truths. Our Western culture has been systematically doing this for nearly two centuries now. We have banished God from what we choose to call 'the real world', and given our credence instead to all manner of myths — social, economic, scientific, political and now also religious, in the form of New Age gods of wood and stone, ie, the natural world itself. Paul's comments on this process are strikingly relevant.

> For although [people] knew God, they neither glorified him as God nor gave thanks to him, but their thinking became futile and their foolish hearts were darkened. Although they claimed to be wise, they became fools and exchanged the glory of the immortal God for images made to look like mortal man and birds and animals and reptiles.
>
> *Romans 1:21–23*

As Christians living in such a world, we have to be prepared to face up to its blasphemy. That means more than having to tolerate bad language in the workplace. The kind of implicit blasphemies of the world around us, as we saw above, are much more serious than habits of speech. For our society as a whole, having refused to honour God, bows down to a host of other idols. It is a hard tide to stand against. If things are going well, then the Christian will be the butt of questions and taunts about the irrelevance of his old-fashioned belief in God. If disaster strikes, he may well find himself bearing the brunt of accusations against God for allowing such things to happen. It is typically human to take credit for success and to blame God for disaster. It is also typically atheist to blame the God one doesn't believe exists for things he should not have allowed if he did exist.

But we cannot get away with only pointing the finger at the fallen world. Do we as Christians learn from the lessons we know full well, or give due honour to the God who holds our lives and all our ways in his hands? 'Though you knew all this' (Daniel 5:22) is a terrifying phrase. The finger of God has given us the commandments, and the word of God has given us many illustrations of the danger of ignoring them. Though we know full well (ever since David and Bathsheba) the dangerous consequences of adultery, more and more Christian marriages are hurt and often shattered by it. Though we know (ever since Achan, and from the warnings of Christ himself) of the horrid sin of covetousness, we still flirt with the gods of materialism and greed along with the rest of our society while three quarters of the world go hungry. Though we know how much importance God gives to truth and integrity, we still pollute our churches with gossip, broken confidences, bickering and false accusations. Though we know that dishonest weights and measures literally stink in God's nostrils (as an 'abomination'), we still compromise with dodgy professional deals, and justify questionable and unfair practices on the grounds that 'business is business'.

I sometimes shiver to think of some apocalyptic

video recording of *all that we know* from the Bible, history and experience, played on a split screen alongside *all that we do or don't do* in spite of what we know. 'But you . . . have not humbled yourself, though you knew all this . . . you did not honour [God].' May God save us from such a judgment.

And so at last to the interpretation of three enigmatic words.

This is the inscription that was written:

MENE, MENE, TEKEL, PARSIN

This is what these words mean:

Mene: God has numbered the days of your reign and brought it to an end.
Tekel: You have been weighed in the scales and found wanting.
Peres: Your kingdom is divided and given to the Medes and Persians.   *Daniel 5:25–28*

The three words on the wall literally meant a mina, a shekel, and a half, which were three descending values of coin, but in Daniel's alternative reading of the roots of the words they meant numbered, weighed, divided. This was the verdict on Belshazzar and his kingdom. The honour and office conferred on Daniel (v 29), in all its drunken hollowness, lasted scarcely a few hours.

That very night Belshazzar king of the Babylonians was slain, and Darius the Mede took over the kingdom at the age of sixty-two.   *Daniel 5:30*

THE MYSTERY OF PROVIDENCE

Daniel 4 and 5 leave us with an unanswered question regarding the dealings of God in human history. They have certainly answered the question of who rules: God does, and all human authority is subject to him. Both chapters have reinforced that fundamental biblical affirmation. But the question can still be asked as to why Nebuchadnezzar and Belshazzar were treated so very differently. Why humble the one into repentance, grace and restoration, but humiliate the other with merely a few hours' notice of his doom and destruction?

The text gives no real answer, except for the fact of Nebuchadnezzar's repentance and Belshazzar's deliberate rejection of the knowledge he had. Yet outwardly, humanly, as far as matters of public observance went, they were both state authorities, both were secular rulers, both were autocrats, both were proud.

So consider the role of Daniel in relation to them both. He was a public servant of both, and also considered that he was serving the God of heaven by serving both. Furthermore he was called to be faithful to the demands of the word of God as it was revealed to him in relation to both of them. To Nebuchadnezzar he had to give a warning and a challenge to respond, in the hope that he could avert judgment – a word which, as we saw, enabled Nebuchadnezzar to find restoration after judgment. To Belshazzar, however, he had to give an unequivocal word of irreversible doom. No warning. No appeal. Presumably the time of patience and possible repentance was long past.

How did Daniel know the difference? How did he know what the word of God was in each situation? I suspect that once again it had something to do with his thrice-daily prayer life in the midst of his busy administrative duties. I wonder if, in fact, it was out of that prayer life, combined with his public office, that the sharp edge of Daniel's true mission was forged. As we said before, he was not a prophet in the true sense. Yet he was called on these occasions to deliver the word of God, plainly stated to the point of extreme discomfort, right into the very heart of government.

Now we know from Daniel 7 onwards that Daniel was privy to more insights into God's dealings in history and the spiritual meaning of the contemporary affairs of his day than any of us are likely to 'enjoy'. But even if we never have visions like his (which is a relief as far as I'm concerned!) we *can* emulate both his life of persistent prayer, and his bold faith in affirming the superiority of the reign of God over all human authorities.

At any time, the secular authorities under which we have to live and work and carry on our Christian mission may become a Nebuchadnezzar or a Belshazzar. Our task is to get on with the job God has given us to do, but to be ready at any time with the word of witness, with pastoral warning or prophetic protest, undergirded by constant prayer. And we must be prepared to be treated to extremes. Belshazzar's response (civic honours and high praise) is unlikely to be much repeated. The lion's den of Daniel 6 seems more probable in today's world, or, most often of all in our wearily cynical society, we are likely simply to be paralysed by waves of hostile, suffocating apathy.

6
FACING
THE
LIONS

My wife says she never saw me really angry till we went to India! I am normally a fairly placid person, not given to great extremes of emotion at the upper or lower ends of the scale. Anger and I are not often found in each other's company, for any length of time at least. But it was there, in a Christian institution, that I experienced for the first time in my life the nastiness of being misunderstood. I mean seriously, not just because of my Ulster accent! The circumstances no longer matter now, and indeed I can scarcely remember them, but it was one of those issues in a community where administrative breakdowns are compounded with personal short-comings and animosities, and then inflated by pride and the fear of losing face. Things were said and done which lacked integrity in themselves and did injustice to some people. I was drawn into it unavoidably because of official responsibilities I held. Then I found that my motives were misinterpreted. I heard about things being said about me in senior meetings. My family also were a target of criticism. I felt stung and went through a time of serious anger, some of which got expressed and some carefully concealed. It was a time of feeling the pressure of being a victim, of being 'got at', of proverbial stabbings in the back. It was not, in short, very nice.

If that's the worst such experience of personal animosity that I go through in life, I shall, of course, be a very fortunate man. Although it was nasty, it was at least moderated by the Christian environment. But it gave me some tiny insight into the kind of pressures that Christians live under in the pagan, secular world when they are subjected to the hatreds and spite of others. The proverb about being thrown into 'a den of lions' is not at all an exaggerated metaphor for what some believers face in our world.

One of the most powerful sermons I have heard or read on Daniel 6 was by a Kenyan bishop whose outspoken condemnation of social and political injustice in his country made him a target of government attacks. He has not only received death threats, but has on one occasion been attacked along with his family in his own home by thugs sent to kill him. Like the Daniel he had only just preached on, he was delivered from death. Other Christians, however, including a fellow bishop, have died for their convictions.

So Daniel 6 has a very sharp relevance to all Christians who are put under pressure by authorities, especially in those parts of the world where to stand up for the living God can be a matter of life or death.

Daniel had survived the collapse of the Babylonian empire, and had now risen to the higher ranks of civil administration in the Persian empire that replaced it. As they say, governments come and governments go, but civil servants go on for ever. By this time he was a very old man, yet once again we find him subjected to a severe test of his faithfulness to God, a test even more searching than anything he faced as a young student in Nebuchadnezzar's academy.

That Daniel faced this challenge to his faith in old age is a sobering lesson. There never comes a time in life when we can sit back and think that our faithfulness to God is so well established that it will never be challenged or tested again. I have always been impressed with the wisdom of Joshua who, when he himself was an old man, addressed the assembly of those who had shared in the conquest with him many years earlier, and challenged them to 'choose for yourselves *this day* whom you will serve' (Joshua 24:15; cf 23:1, 2). Yesterday's covenant loyalty was not enough. Today calls for a fresh choice. When did you last actually *choose* to serve God, in any situation where there was a real alternative?

DANIEL'S EXCELLENCE

It pleased Darius to appoint 120 satraps to rule throughout the kingdom, with three administrators over them, one of whom was Daniel. The satraps were made accountable to them so that the king might not suffer loss. Now Daniel so distinguished himself among the administrators and the satraps by his exceptional qualities that the king planned to set him over the whole kingdom. At this, the

administrators and the satraps tried to find grounds
for charges against Daniel in his conduct of
government affairs, but they were unable to do so.
They could find no corruption in him, because he
was trustworthy and neither corrupt nor negligent.

Daniel 6:1–4

Like a certain British comedian, Daniel could have said,
'I didn't get where I am today by negligence and unre-
liability.' Nor had he got where he was by luck, by
belonging to a privileged elite by birth (quite the reverse
– he had overcome the disadvantage of his racial and
social background), or even by royal or divine favourit-
ism. The opening verses of this chapter intentionally
leave us in no doubt that Daniel's high position was
thoroughly deserved and appropriate to his high qualities as a person. Two things stand out.

● *His personal ability.* Daniel was outstanding. This
simple fact is expressed in the phrase 'his exceptional
qualities'. Literally it means he had 'an excellent spirit'.
He himself, and all that he did, were noticeably distinguished by a superior quality. He was a man of great
natural gifts which were being thoroughly used through
consistently applied hard work. The qualities which had
brought him to the notice of king Nebuchadnezzar had
not been the brief, bright flare of a young academic
egghead who could mug it all up for exams, but who
would then fizzle out under the pressures of real life in
the rough world of politics. Daniel was 'cabinet' quality,
and 'top-drawer of the cabinet' as well, if the pun is
forgivable!

● *His personal integrity.* This is the vital other side of the story. Sometimes people of great ability lack integrity, and so their gifts are used corruptly. The financial world has been shaken in recent years by the almost incredible frauds that have been perpetrated by extremely clever people, people whose enormous expertise has been bent to facilitate greed and theft on a grand scale. In the political world, we have witnessed Watergate and 'Irangate' and, in Britain, the shame of council housing rackets in which corrupt officials, whose job is to provide for the needy, actually exploit them for their own pockets. Doubtless the administration of a bureaucracy as vast as Persia's provided men in Daniel's position with plenty of scope for similar scams in the ancient world.

But Daniel was trustworthy. He could be trusted by those below him, ie, the people he served, since he could not be bent or corrupted by higher officials to work against their interests. And he could be trusted by those above him, ie, the king himself, that he would not be bribed or bought by any court conspirators or corrupt officials. So even his enemies could find no sniff of corruption.

However, it was not just that he was not corrupt. He was not negligent either. There are some people who are pretty harmless, but only because they are too lazy to be anything else. We all know the kind of officials in public offices who are infuriating not because they are doing wrong, but because they are doing nothing. Seats are kept warm and paper shuffles around desks, but nothing moves in the real world. Daniel was not one of these. Things got done. He was 'not negligent'. So for both reasons – his ability and his integrity – the king knew that with Daniel in charge, he would not suffer loss. Here was a man who could be trusted to get the job done.

From the perspective of the story in Daniel 6, the point of dwelling on these characteristics of Daniel himself is clear. It is to underline the fact that his persecution and testing was entirely unjust. There is a Job-like quality about him in this story. In the book of Job we are invited to contemplate a man who was as righteous as we could imagine, but who suffered the worst calamities we could imagine because of things he knew nothing about and had no control over. Here we see a man who is the perfect model of excellence, in both practical and moral terms, who nevertheless suffers unjust hatred and attack.

In fact, the irony of the story is that he was put under such pressure by the very state he was serving so well. As Daniel later pointed out, courteously but powerfully (in view of where he said it from), he was not only innocent in the sight of God, but he had never done the state any harm either (v 22). That was a massive understatement! He had done the state more good through his honest and efficient administration than all his enemies put together. And still he suffered. Even more remarkably, *after* his brush with the lions, he went on serving the state. He did not hand in his resignation in a fit of righteous indignation. Just as he modelled in advance the saying of Jesus about loving our enemies, so he is an example of what Peter encouraged Christians of his day to do. Even if you suffer for doing good, he said, endure it patiently, *and go on doing good.*

Submit yourselves for the Lord's sake to every
authority instituted among men . . . For it is God's
will that by doing good you should silence the
ignorant talk of foolish men.   *1 Peter 2:13, 15*

Who is going to harm you if you are eager to do
good? But even if you should suffer for what is right,
you are blessed. 'Do not fear what they fear; do not
be frightened.' But in your hearts set apart Christ as
Lord. Always be prepared to give an answer to
everyone who asks you to give the reason for the
hope that you have. But do this with gentleness and
respect, keeping a clear conscience, so that those
who speak maliciously against your good behaviour
in Christ may be ashamed of their slander. It is
better, if it is God's will, to suffer for doing good
than for evil.   *1 Peter 3:13–17*

However, if you suffer as a Christian, do not be
ashamed, but praise God that you bear that
name . . .
    So then, those who suffer according to God's
will should commit themselves to their faithful
Creator and continue to do good.   *1 Peter 4:16, 19*

There is another point worth noting here. All Daniel's
ability and integrity had been put at the disposal of this
secular, pagan, political authority. Apart from his daily
prayer, we know nothing about Daniel's personal or
religious life. We don't know if he was involved in any
kind of social or religious good causes. We don't know
if he was a prominent lay leader in his local synagogue.
What we are told is that in his daily secular job he was
the very best. Even apart from the rest of the story and
its major point, that is worth taking to heart.

It is a very sad thing if Christians have the idea that a secular job is just a means of keeping the body fed and clothed, and therefore feel at liberty to invest just enough of their ability and effort to keep the job. Then they reckon they can save their best for 'God's work'. Such a dichotomy betrays a failure to see the whole of life as 'God's work'. By contrast, Paul urged even slaves who were believers to work hard and honestly for their masters – even non-Christian masters – on the basis that in doing so they were in reality serving the Lord Christ

> Slaves, obey your earthly masters in everything; and do it, not only when their eye is on you and to win their favour, but with sincerity of heart and reverence for the Lord. Whatever you do, work at it with all your heart, as working for the Lord, not for men, since you know that you will receive an inheritance from the Lord as a reward. It is the Lord Christ you are serving. *Colossians 3:22–24*

The college where I teach is in the business of training and equipping people for cross-cultural life in Christian mission. When people apply to come here as students, we ask for at least three letters of reference – one from a personal friend, one from a church minister or leader, and one from a secular employer (most of our students have already been working in some secular professional capacity). Before interviewing candidates, I always look with greatest interest at the third reference. You can expect that a person's Christian friends and pastor will say nice things about them (though we hope they 'speak the truth in love'!), but I want to know what impression they have made in the *non-Christian* workplace. Have they been reliable, honest, hard-working? Do they relate well to colleagues? Are they known for doing a good job? Because if there are question marks over the way they work in secular life, what guarantee is there that they will be any different in the pressures of Christian work? What warms my heart most is when the employer's reference says something to the effect that, although they respect their employee's decision and sense of vocation, they really wish he or she was not leaving because they will be such a loss to the place. If this candidate is really going to be missed, then I know we've got somebody worth having!

The example of Daniel's excellence, therefore, challenges us to think hard about our daily lives as Christians in the world. On the one hand it warns us not to be surprised (as Peter and James wrote) if we experience unfairness and injustice in the way we are treated. On the other hand it searches our motives and integrity in the way we actually do our work in the secular sphere.

DANIEL'S ENEMIES

At this, the administrators and the satraps tried to find grounds for charges against Daniel in his conduct of government affairs, but they were unable to do so. They could find no corruption in him, because he was trustworthy and neither corrupt nor negligent. Finally these men said, 'We will never find any basis for charges against this man Daniel unless it has something to do with the law of his God.'

Daniel 6:4, 5

It is very common in life that those who are good and able arouse the dislike of those who are neither. It's just one of the many perversities of human nature. The nursery tale of The Ugly Duckling (like many nursery tales and rhymes) illustrates a truth of experience. Nobody likes somebody who is different from the comfortable crowd, who is not 'one of us'. Especially if the difference is over a matter of morality, or anything that threatens to show up what is really going on. So this account of how such a competent man as Daniel had such nasty enemies is a mirror of the real life experience of many people.

Their hatred

What made them hate Daniel so much? The text gives some hints at the reasons behind their malicious thinking and tactics.

• *Jealousy*. They heard about Daniel's promotion (Daniel 6:3). There was a leak from the royal cabinet: somebody who had the confidence of the king's counsel told his colleagues about the king's intention to promote Daniel to the top job as head of the whole civil administration, so an acute epidemic of professional jealousy sets in. Political life is, of course, an incubator for this kind of jealousy. We know how much we groan with cynicism as we watch modern day politicians jostling for the limelight, the best photo-opportunity, the catchiest sound-bite, the plummiest jobs. Sentimental lip-service is paid to the ideals of public service and false modesty is knee-deep, but the reality is a rat-race for power and influence, and/or the benefits in terms of wealth or prestige that may follow.

But Christians and Christian institutions are not at all immune to the ravages of professional jealousy. Churches and denominations sometimes have their 'career structure', their hierarchy (the very word is out of tune with a biblical view of ministry). I could never bear the fact that after ordination I would be asked questions about my ambition in the clerical life – by well-meaning people, of course, but with such a distorted view of ministry. Why are clergy appointments called 'preferment'? Why are bishops 'enthroned'? And while I could not set out a logical defence of the way bishops are appointed in the Church of England, I shudder at the alternative methods of election that prevail in other parts of the Anglican communion and other episcopal churches, having seen at close quarters in India the horrific abuses it invites including vote-swaying, bribery and corruption of all sorts, even physical violence – all in the scramble for a top job that gives access to the levers of power and personal gain.

• *Racism.* Daniel's enemies decided to attack him in relation to his religion ('the law of his God') but, of course, that was not merely a matter of private belief. It was his ethnic identity as well. Their racist attitude is betrayed by the way they describe him to the king in verse 13: 'one of the exiles from Judah'. This incident takes place more than fifty years after the Jews had been forcibly brought to Babylon. Jews had settled down there now for two generations. Many, like Daniel, were thoroughly integrated into the country's social and political system, after a comprehensive academic and cultural re-education (as we saw in Daniel 1). Yet these hostile officials still refer to him in terms probably as derogatory as calling second and third generation black British citizens 'immigrants'. Daniel 6 is not just a spiritual tale of courage in the face of danger. It carries an unmistakeable whiff of anti-Semitism and thus unmasks the twisted face of racism.

If it is hard to tolerate someone else getting promotion, it is even harder if that person comes from a despised ethnic group or social class or regional background, or is just the wrong gender. Then personal jealousy is linked to group pride, and all our human instinct to protect the in-group from the outsider surges up.

In the 1992 General Election in Britain, John Taylor, a black Christian, stood as the Conservative candidate in Cheltenham – normally a very safe Conservative seat. Though he was very well qualified for the job, there was a row when he was selected as a candidate, and the racist attitudes of those who opposed him were not even concealed. He was defeated in the election by a small margin, and it was very clear that it was the racism of a group within his own party that had engineered his defeat. Afterwards he described the whole experience as having been like Daniel in the lion's den.

• *Spite*. Jesus once said that people love darkness because their deeds are evil, so they hate the light. Goodness is not popular, unless it coincides with the self-interest of others. Since it usually threatens to expose those who are evil, they will seek to stifle it to protect themselves. These officials probably realized that if Daniel was promoted to the top of the civil administration, then it would be difficult for them to carry on their own corrupt practices. They could be exposed and dismissed. So their reaction is to do their utmost to drag Daniel down to their own level – to get *him* dismissed on a charge of corruption before he can expose theirs. They knew all about 'negative campaigning', about muck-raking. They knew the tactics of the gutter press. However, finally they had to admit defeat. Nothing would stick to Daniel. His record was so clean that any charges would be so lacking in credibility that it would make his accusers look foolish.

'Do not be surprised,' warns the New Testament. We live in a world which is in rebellion against God and will, therefore, show all the marks of that rebellion when faced with anyone who stands for the values of God's kingdom – truth, honesty, integrity, goodness, and even plain competence. Such things are not welcome in our world.

Their methods

● *They exploited his strength.* Since they could find no chink in Daniel's armour, they decided to trap him in the armour itself. Having failed to find a weakness, they decided to engineer his downfall by using his own strength against him. They asked what it was that was most distinctive about Daniel. What mattered most to him? They realized that above and behind all his excellent work record was this fact of his loyalty to his God. There was no conflict in practice between this loyalty and his obvious loyalty and service to the state, but if they could set up a situation in which they would force a conflict, then his strength of religious conviction would bring about his own downfall. It was brilliant.

In fact, it was diabolically clever. For the tactics of Satan are often like this. In the early days of a Christian's life, he can have a field day tripping us up through our weaknesses – old habits, ingrained personality traits, attitudes and prejudices that haven't been converted yet, simple ignorance of the Bible's teaching, or lack of good advice and guidance on how to live as a Christian. But as a Christian grows up, by teaching, experience and God's grace, these weaknesses are tackled. New, Christlike qualities begin to take their place. Now of course it is never true that we shed all our weaknesses. It would be daft as well as ignorant to imagine that. But, by the grace of God and the fruit of his Spirit, our weaknesses are turned into strengths – and Satan changes tack. If he cannot pull us down by obvious and 'easy' temptations and sins, he will use the very things we thought were our strengths or our gifts, to trap us into situations where we end up flat on our face again in sin and defeat.

For example, being a Christian strengthens a young person's sense of responsibility towards parents, since that is a clear part of biblical and Christian duty. So let that newly reinforced commitment to respect and obedience grow and develop till it becomes a definite, conscious virtue. Then see to it that the strength of that commitment is thrown into conflict with loyalty to the call of Christ himself. An Indian woman among my students found this an intolerable tension in her young life as a newly converted Christian in a Hindu home. She wanted to obey her parents in all things, yet could not yield to their severe and prolonged pressure to give up her loyalty to Jesus as her only God and Lord, and worship the Hindu deities with them. With God's help, she stood firm, but the sharpness of the temptation was that, by giving in to their demands, she would not have seemed to be doing anything immoral, but quite the reverse – she would have seemed to be fulfilling the duties of an obedient daughter.

It is a sad fact that many Christian pastors fall into sexual temptations that arise out of the very nature of their work. A survey conducted by the journal *Christianity Today* discovered that twelve per cent of those who responded to a questionnaire distributed to a thousand pastors admitted having had sexual intercourse in the course of their pastoral work. Eighteen per cent admitted to more general sexual involvement. It is not likely that these men and women went into the job with the intention of doing so. Most, if not all of them, probably never imagined at the start of their pastoral ministry that they would ever become entangled in this way. Yet they fell, their feet of clay tripped up by the very thing that was their gift and strength – a pastoral heart; a caring spirit, but careless eyes. This is not in any sense to excuse such behaviour, but to point out that it may be tangled up with a person's strong points, in just the way that Satan can exploit.

The message is, don't only guard your weak points. Watch your strong points as well. Satan knows how to attack both.

● *They violated the constitution.*

> So the administrators and the satraps went as a group to the king and said: 'O King Darius, live for ever!

> The royal administrators, prefects, satraps, advisers and governors have all agreed that the king should issue an edict and enforce the decree that anyone who prays to any god or man during the next thirty days, except to you, O king, shall be thrown into the lions' den. Now, O king, issue the decrée and put it in writing so that it cannot be altered – in accordance with the laws of the Medes and Persians, which cannot be repealed.' So King Darius put the decree in writing.
>
> *Daniel 6:6–9*

The proposal they put to the king was very flattering. It had to be, because it was only by dazzling him with flattery that they were able to divert attention from the fact that their proposal was quite unconstitutional. Indeed the Persian empire granted a large degree of religious freedom. One of the first acts of Cyrus the Persian (Daniel 1:21; 6:28; Ezra 1:1–11) when he defeated Babylon and took over its whole empire, was to issue an edict liberating captive peoples and their gods. It was this edict which gave the Jews (along with other peoples that had been captured by Babylon) the freedom to return from exile to Jerusalem and to rebuild the temple to Yahweh, their God. The part of Cyrus's edict relevant to the Jews is recorded in Ezra 1:1–4. Full details of his policies are recorded on a stone cylinder, known as the Cyrus Cylinder, which you can see in the British Museum.

Cyrus's idea, which became official colonial policy of the Persian empire, was the opposite of Assyrian and Babylonian policy before him. They had taken the view that the best way to keep nations subject to the imperial power was to disrupt them, to disperse and deport populations, and especially to capture their gods by bringing their idols to the capital city. Yahweh had no idol, so, as we saw at the beginning of the book of Daniel, Nebuchadnezzar brought other sacred vessels from the Jerusalem temple instead. Cyrus seems to have considered that such a policy was a recipe for constant discontent and rebellion. Why keep all the gods cooped up in your capital city, where they would get angry with you, when you could release them all back to their homes? Build nice temples for them, and then your subject peoples would be grateful to you, pray to their gods for you, and you'd have a peaceful, contented empire.

The official policy of the Persian empire, therefore, was to grant relative religious freedom to its subject peoples, within the limits of overall loyalty to the Persian state itself. In this respect it was a more liberal regime that its predecessors. Constitutionally, therefore, there was no reason why, in Daniel's case or for any of the Jews, the requirements of 'the law of his God' should have come into conflict with 'the laws of the Medes and Persians'. But his enemies succeeded in what amounted to a temporary suspension of the constitution in order to engineer precisely such a conflict. They knew that if they forced Daniel to choose between the law of his God and the law of the state, he would choose his God. They could only force such a choice by changing the law. So they went to Darius to do just that. But they concealed their negative intention (to destroy Daniel) under a charade of positive flattery (to honour the king). Doubtless they threw in some other supporting arguments.

'We need to encourage harmony and unity among all the races of our empire. So our proposal will be good for race relations.' (There is a large poster in Bombay airport, and other public locations in India, that proclaims: 'Whether Hindu, Muslim, Christian, Sikh or Jain, we are Indians first and Indians last.')

'It's all right for people to have their own religion privately and locally, but everyone must acknowledge that loyalty to the king and the state comes first.'

'There's really only one patriotic religion and everybody should acknowledge that for a while, even if they go back to their own religions afterwards.'

And the king bought it. Fooled by the flattery, he rubber-stamped the new bill so that it became law, without further consultation or reflection. The rest of the story makes it clear that he later regretted his hasty decision. However the deed was done; the constitution was effectively suspended by a law which was itself unconstitutional, and it gave the enemies of Daniel enough time to bring him down under a cloak of legality.

We need to be on our guard as Christians and as citizens with regard to the constitutional framework of our countries. If we believe that all human authority is delegated authority, entrusted by God; if we believe that basic human rights and constitutional freedoms reflect God's moral will and are for the good of all people; if, in other words, our biblical faith tells us something about our humanity and not just about our Christianity; then we of all people must stand up for constitutional rights and freedoms.

We are all aware of how human rights in general are violated in many parts of the world. We know about the struggles that Christians face in many countries where the law itself discriminates against them. However, even if we live in a so-called secular democracy, we need to watch out for the subtle ways in which the enemies of the Christian faith will undermine or remove the precious freedom to worship and witness.

In India in the 1970s a number of states in the Indian union passed 'Freedom of Religion' bills. Contrary to the impression given by the title, the meaning of these acts was that people were free to have their own religion, but *not* to convert anyone from another religion to their own, or indeed to convert to another religion voluntarily, without very long and complicated legal processes. In a few states, these laws have survived and are used harshly against Christians. This is in spite of the fact that they can be shown to be contrary to Article 25 of the Fundamental Rights section of the Indian constitution, which guarantees the 'the right freely to profess, practice *and propagate* religion'.

Indeed, there are powerful movements of Hindu 'fundamentalism' in India which would prefer India to have a constitution more like the one that used to govern Nepal, which stated (in terms that echo the law signed by Darius in Daniel 6),

> 'No person shall propagate Christianity, Islam or any other faith so as to disrupt the traditional religion of the Hindu community in Nepal, or to convert any adherent of the Hindu religion into these faiths.'

Prison sentences of three to six years were imposed for violation of this law. It is ironic that Nepal, until recently the only constitutionally Hindu country in the world, has moved to a more secular constitution, whereas India, with its secular constitution, is under pressure to move in the opposite direction.

In Singapore, since 1990, a 'Religious Harmony Law' restricts evangelism by any religion, because of the desire to keep the peace between the Muslim, Hindu and Christian communities, especially in view of the amazingly rapid growth of the Christian church there in the last decade.

But these places are far away, people in Britain might think. Surely nothing like that will ever happen here, with our strong tradition of democratic freedoms. We should not be complacent. Notice that the kind of legislation that restricts evangelism is always labelled something to do with 'freedom' or 'harmony'. I heard recently that a church in Australia was requested to remove a placard saying 'Jesus is Lord', on the grounds that it was a racist statement. This could well be the line on which restrictions in Britain might be advocated. Nobody would suggest banning Christianity, or anything so crude. But we might be told that any form of evangelism, especially among communities of other faiths, is detrimental to racial or community harmony, and therefore it should be declared illegal. We are already told by some powerful voices that any claim to know the truth, or any assertion of the uniqueness of Christ as Lord and Saviour, are offensive to other religions. It would not be an enormous step to move from that to a prohibition on any form of evangelism which made such claims, however humbly and sensitively.

Are we on our guard first of all to do everything within our democratic power to prevent such a move, and secondly, if such a situation were forced upon us, to know how to respond to it? Among other things, it would force us to listen and learn from the great majority of Christians around the world who do in fact live and witness in the midst of such restrictions.

And it would drive us back to learn again from Daniel, a man whose loyalty to the state is now thrown into conflict with his loyalty to God. It is worth noting, in view of what we have just been discussing, that the test for Daniel had to do with something being *forbidden*, not something being *required* (as in the case of Shadrach, Meschach and Abednego in Daniel 3). In some ways, if the state orders you to do something that you know God forbids, it is a simple matter (though costly!) to refuse. But if the state merely tells you to stop doing something, it is rather easier to go along with it, especially if, as is the case with evangelism, we weren't doing a great deal of it to start with!

Who would have noticed if Daniel had stopped praying for a month? Could he not have prayed silently and secretly? But to do that would have been to sell out to precisely the idolatry that the state was demanding. If the state begins to make claims that amount to divine status, then even prayer becomes a political act, because in prayer, especially public, visible prayer, you are affirming the reality of a higher authority than the state. You are appealing *beyond* Caesar. You are denying the claims of the state to have ultimate power and authority over you.

This is why, in the New Testament, instructions to Christians to submit to political authorities is linked to the command to *pray* for them. Prayer puts political authorities in perspective. If you pray for kings and governments, then you are automatically seeing them in their proper, subordinate place – under the rule and control of the God you are praying to. I believe, as I've said before, that Daniel was praying for Darius, just as he had been praying for Nebuchadnezzar and Babylon, according to the instructions of Jeremiah (Jeremiah 29:7). And this is why he refused to stop praying, even when the same Darius ordered him to. Daniel's prayer life kept him in touch with a higher authority than Darius, and no edict would change that, not even 'the laws of the Medes and Persians'.

DANIEL'S VALUES

> Now when Daniel learned that the decree had been published, he went home to his upstairs room where the windows opened towards Jerusalem. Three times a day he got down on his knees and prayed, giving thanks to his God, just as he had done before.
>
> *Daniel 6:10*

Daniel's lifetime of disciplined, regular, habitual prayer probably meant that it would have been more difficult to stop praying than to carry on. Some features of his prayer life are mentioned almost incidentally, yet in such a way as to show us that it was not something bizarre or abnormal. He prayed three times a day, he got down on his knees, he gave thanks to God, he asked God for help (vs 10, 11). All simple things that any of us could imitate.

It shows the desperation of his enemies and the evil depths of their determination to get him out of the way, that they had him arraigned for such activity. Not only was it no threat to the king (Daniel's loyalty to the state could not be questioned), but in fact, if the king but knew, it was probably to the king's benefit since almost certainly part of Daniel's prayer was *for* the king. The prayer of God's people is for the good of the world, not just the church, which adds to the tragic irony of the trap Darius fell into. He had to stop someone doing something which was actually for his own benefit!

But what about those windows in the room where Daniel prayed, the windows 'opened towards Jerusalem'? It is hardly accidental that they are mentioned here, just as it is hardly accidental that Daniel chose to pray in this room with west-facing windows. Was it simply superstition, or nostalgia?

I remember as a young student in Cambridge, suffering the heartache of separation from my girlfriend, how the window of my room faced roughly north west, and how I used to gaze out of it thinking of all the miles between me and her in Belfast, and wishing I could beam across them in an instant to see her (then beam back and finish the essay I should have been doing!). I don't think Daniel, now in his eighties, was gazing out the window in that frame of mind.

There were probably two reasons why Daniel chose to pray towards Jerusalem. First, because of his deep knowledge of the scriptures (cf. Daniel 9:2). The record of Solomon's prayer at the dedication of the temple in 1 Kings refers a lot to people praying 'towards' the city, or the temple, or the land.

> . . . if [your people] turn back with you will all their heart and soul in the land of their enemies who took them captive, and pray to you towards the land you

gave their fathers, towards the city you have chosen
and the temple I have built for your Name; then
from heaven, your dwelling place, hear their prayer
and their plea, and uphold their cause.

1 Kings 8:48, 49

We know from Daniel 9 that this was exactly the
burden of Daniel's heart. So, in praying towards Jerusalem at windows opened in that direction, he was
simply doing what his scriptures said. Daniel was a man
of the Bible as well as a man of prayer.

But a second, deeper reason is that this action
reveals the whole orientation and inspiration of Daniel's
life. Here he was, living, working, serving for all his
adult life in Babylon, the city of Nebuchadnezzar and
his successors. But all the time he was looking, praying,
meditating, 'turning', towards Jerusalem, the city of
God. He drew from it the identity, character and values
of his own life. Jerusalem, to the Jews, was not merely
an attractive hill-top city, not even merely their capital
city. In fact, it was not really a very impressive city at
all, as world cities go, even in those days. But it was
the place where Yahweh, God of Israel had made his
name to dwell. The presence of God was there in the
temple, the law of God was known and proclaimed
there. So, although it often failed in reality, it was supposed to be the place where God's righteousness and
justice were modelled.

Jerusalem was the place to which, in prophetic
vision, the nations would come to learn about the true
God and his ways (Isaiah 2:1–5). It was the focal point
of the messianic hope and of God's future reign. God
would one day rule from Zion – Jerusalem, even Jeru-

salem in ruins (as it was through most of Daniel's life, although by the time of Daniel 6 it was being re-settled), symbolized all that. Jerusalem, though physically flattened, reminded Daniel of the kingdom of his God, past, present and future. To pray 'towards Jerusalem', then, was to align himself in the direction of God and his purposes and values. It was like taking a daily compass bearing for his life, enabling him to set everything else in its true perspective in relation to the reality of God.

So, for Daniel, the key to the future, and all the purposes of God, the meaning of life and his ultimate values, lay not in the city Nebuchadnezzar had built, but in the city Nebuchadnezzar had destroyed. Daniel lived in the midst of the dazzling imperial culture of the capital city of the most powerful world empire. He rubbed shoulders with the great, the wealthy and the powerful. He walked the corridors of earthly power and glory. Yet every day, three times a day, he got down on his knees and thought about God and Jerusalem. He kept his orientation right. Prayer reminded him of his true values. Prayer 'towards Jerusalem' re-aligned his busy political life in the direction of God's will and commands. Prayer was the means by which Daniel was able to be a faithful and honest servant of one of the kingdoms of this world and, at the same time, serve the kingdom of God. He lived in Zion not when he got to heaven, but in the midst of the ambiguous, complex and potentially bestial (see Daniel 7) world of human power politics.

So when I think of those open windows, I don't see them as an escape hatch, but as an entry shaft. That is, they were not so much to let Daniel's prayers out as to let the God of Jerusalem in. Daniel's prayer life was not escapism *from* the daily grind of political administration. Rather it was his means of bringing the power and presence of God *into* his immediate work. Daniel was God's salt and light in the secular world in which he moved. His saltiness was preserved and his lamp kept polished by his daily contact with their source, God himself.

Whatever our personal pattern of devotional life, it is worth asking the question, how does it relate to the everyday real world of secular life and work? Is it a moment of blessed relief and escape from it? Or is it the means of drawing the presence of God – with all his values and priorities – into that world? This applies not only to our private prayers, but also to our participation in Sunday worship and our times of fellowship, prayer or Bible study with other Christians. Are they evasive or invasive? Escapist or transformative? Let's make sure the windows are 'open towards Jerusalem', that we daily re-orientate our lives in the direction of God's name, God's will, God's purposes, God's direction. Like Daniel, yet again a model of one of Jesus's commands, let's 'seek first the kingdom of God and his justice'.

DANIEL'S VINDICATION

The rest of the story of this chapter is the familiar bit! Certainly it's the bit that goes down best with the Sunday school children.

> Then these men went as a group and found Daniel praying and asking God for help. So they went to the king and spoke to him about his royal decree:

'Did you not publish a decree that during the next thirty days anyone who prays to any god or man except to you, O king, would be thrown into the lions' den?'

The king answered, 'The decree stands – in accordance with the laws of the Medes and Persians, which cannot be repealed.'

Then they said to the king, 'Daniel, who is one of the exiles from Judah, pays no attention to you, O king, or to the decree you put in writing. He still prays three times a day.' When the king heard this, he was greatly distressed; he was determined to rescue Daniel and made every effort until sundown to save him.

Then the men went as a group to the king and said to him, 'Remember, O king, that according to the law of the Medes and Persians no decree or edict that the king issues can be changed.'

So the king gave the order, and they brought Daniel and threw him into the lions' den. The king said to Daniel, 'May your God, whom you serve continually, rescue you!'   *Daniel 6:11–16*

The art of the Hebrew story-teller brilliantly brings out the shocked dismay of the king when he realized how cunningly he had been trapped. There was a great emphasis on 'law and order' in Persia. Not for nothing did the expression 'the law of the Medes and Persians' become proverbial for hard and fast rules. Now the king finds himself forced to trample on basic human rights in order to maintain a law which itself violated human freedoms. All because he had allowed himself to be hoodwinked by flattery. Flattery, like bribery, blinds the eye of those who need the clearest vision.

And Darius was neither the first nor the last politician to end up in a blind alley, faced with a dilemma brought about by his own self-interest and pride. Not was he the only one to be trapped into sacrificing the innocent but vulnerable, to placate the wicked but influential. Such injustice is the stock in trade of politics, locally, nationally and internationally, to this day.

There is a reminder, too, of Pontius Pilate. He also found himself cornered into denying justice to a man he knew was innocent, in order, in his case, to maintain a peace which was based on oppression and violence. Like Daniel, Jesus accepted the human authority of the ruler, knowing that real power lay elsewhere and Pilate's was only a delegated authority under the actual kingdom of God.

There are also echoes in the story of the resurrection. Early Christian art often portrayed the story of Daniel's deliverance from the den of lions as a prefiguring of the resurrection.

> A stone was brought and placed over the mouth of the den, and the king sealed it with his own signet ring and with the rings of his nobles, so that Daniel's situation might not be changed. Then the king returned to his palace and spent the night without eating and without any entertainment being brought to him. And he could not sleep.
>
> At first light of dawn, the king got up and hurried to the lions' den. When he came near the den, he called to Daniel in an anguished voice, 'Daniel, servant of the living God, has your God, whom you serve continually, been able to rescue you from the lions?'
>
> Daniel answered, 'O king, live forever! My God sent his angel, and he shut the mouths of the lions.

They have not hurt me, because I was found innocent in his sight. Nor have I ever done any wrong before you, O king.'

The king was overjoyed and gave orders to lift Daniel out of the den. And when Daniel was lifted from the den, no wound was found on him, because he had trusted in his God.   *Daniel 6:17–23*

Notice the stone placed over the 'tomb', and the official seal to prevent any tampering with it. Notice the early morning rush to the tomb, followed by the overwhelming discovery of miraculous life in the place of certain and inescapable death. Above all, notice that Daniel is fully vindicated, just as the resurrection was the vindication of Jesus and all he claimed and taught. Daniel's faithfulness and integrity had been tested to the final extreme, and they had been upheld by an unmistakeable divine verdict. He had been faced with a choice between his principles and his personal safety (to put it mildly!), and his principles had been vindicated.

We cannot know whether Daniel could have known in advance that the lions would suffer an acute attack of lockjaw. It may well have been as surprising for him as it doubtless was for the lions. Like his three friends a long time earlier he trusted in God's ability to deliver him, but was probably prepared to pay the final cost of his loyalty to God and leave his ultimate vindication in God's hands.

Standing up for principles, for God's values, for integrity and conscience, can be costly, especially when the vindication of one's stand has to be taken by faith and cannot be guaranteed in advance.

Dave was a payroll manager in a company. He was

able to organize his own schedule in such a way as to avoid working on Sunday. However, the time came when the higher management asked him to work to a different system that not only required him to insist on Sunday working for other staff, but also to do so himself. He refused, and his job was threatened. He still refused, prepared if necessary to lose his job and suffer the consequences. However, he also devised an alternative rota that built proper rest days, including Sundays, into the system for all workers. In the end the management accepted it, and the result was not only a satisfied workforce, but a healthier one, since fewer days were lost due to sickness – real or claimed. Dave's stand was vindicated, in retrospect. At the same time it was a matter of holding on and facing the lions – the sack.

But the real vindication at the end of this story is not merely Daniel's, but of Daniel's God. The testimony of Darius echoes the words of Nebuchadnezzar both when he was amazed by God's deliverance of Shadrach, Meshach and Abednego from the furnace and also when he himself was restored to sanity (Daniel 3 and 4).

> Then King Darius wrote to all the peoples, nations and men of every language throughout the land:
>
> 'May you prosper greatly!
>
> 'I issue a decree that in every part of my kingdom people must fear and reverence the God of Daniel.
>
> 'For he is the living God
>   and he endures for ever;
>   his kingdom will not be destroyed,
>   his dominion will never end.

He rescues and he saves;
    he performs signs and wonders
    in the heavens and on the earth.
He has rescued Daniel
    from the power of the lions.'   *Daniel 6:25–27*

The irony of this proclamation is that here was a man who had allowed himself and his state to be set up as the ultimate kingdom to which all his subjects must bow and pray, yet now he orders everybody in *his* kingdom to acknowledge a higher kingdom than his own.

That is the final reality to which this book points. Daniel 7 goes on to reinforce the point through visions portraying the ultimate triumph of God and the people of God through one like a 'son of man', over the bestial arrogance and destructiveness of human kingdoms. Multitudes of Christians, and Jews, as much today as in past centuries, have faced lions – literally and metaphorically. Many have been delivered and vindicated. Many have not, in this life.

But the God of Daniel is still the king of heaven, and of earth. His kingdom still rules the kingdoms of this world. He *can* deliver and often does, but he calls us to faithfulness and integrity in our everyday lives, whatever the cost. He calls us to build our lives on the values of his kingdom, not when we get to heaven, but in the here and now.

If we are also called to the extreme test for doing so, let us pray that we have God's grace to meet it with the courage and conviction of Daniel, confident in that final vindication which is guaranteed in the resurrection of Christ himself.

OTHER BOOKS IN THE SERIES

Pioneers or Settlers? Exodus: Adventurous faith for today (Philip Mohabir)

Hunger for Holiness: Malachi: A call to commitment today (Stephen Gaukroger)

God of New Beginnings: Matthew 1–4 in today's world (Rodger Sainsbury)

Thirsty for God: Matthew 5–7: Jesus' teaching for today (Stephen Gaukroger)

Drawing Power: Living out Acts in today's world (Derek Prime)

People Under Pressure: 2 Corinthians: Strategy for stress (Michael Cole)

Open to Others: Ephesians: Overcoming barriers in today's church (Colin Buchanan)

Growing in Christ: 1 Thessalonians: Steps to Christian maturity (Paul Marsh)

Growing Your Gifts: 2 Timothy: Ministry in today's world (Stephen Gaukroger)